WORLD
HERITAGE
JAPAN

RIVER

BOOKS

WORLD HERITAGE JAPAN

JOHN LANDER

PREFACE BY PICO IYER · INTRODUCTION BY YOKO KAWAGUCHI

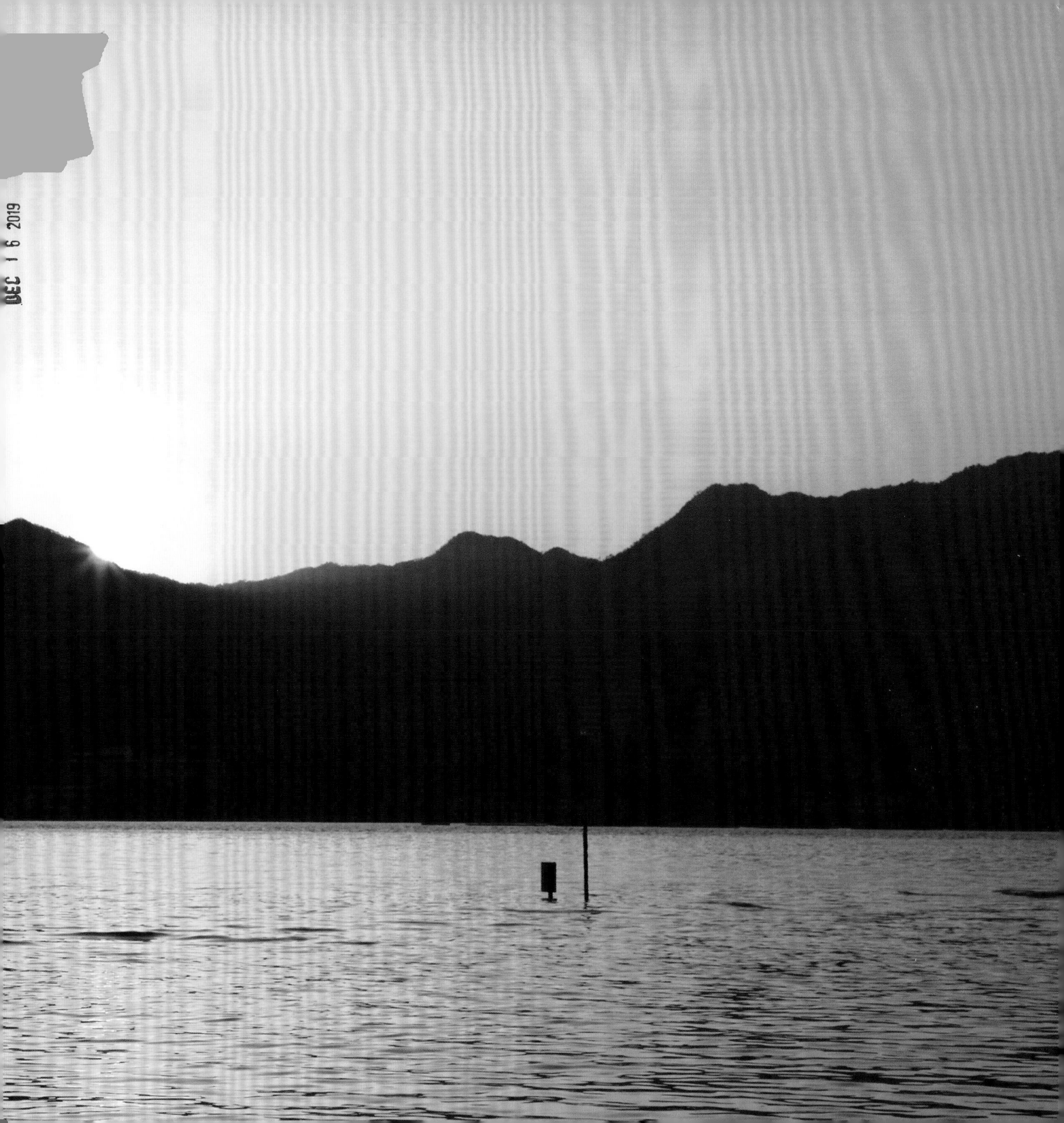

First published in Thailand 2019
by River Books Co., Ltd.
396 Maharaj Road, Tatien
Bangkok 10200 Thailand
Telephone: (66) 2 225-4963
Fax: (66) 2 225-3861
Email: order@riverbooksbk.com
www.riverbooksbk.com

Editor: Narisa Chakrabongse
Production: Paisarn Piemmettawat
Design: Peter Cope / Ruetairat Nanta

ISBN 978 616 451 011 1

Printed and bound in Thailand
by Sirivatana Interprint Public Co., Ltd.

Contents

Preface – Pico Iyer   10
World Heritage Map of Japan   14
Introduction – Yoko Kawaguchi   18
Foreword   20

Nara   24
Kasuga-taisha Shrine   26
Kasugayama Primeval Forest   28
Todaiji   30
Nigatsu-do at Todaiji   32
Kofukuji   33
Hokkiji   34
Horyuji   36
Gangoji   38
Yakushiji   40
Toshodaiji   42
Heijo Palace   44
East Palace Garden Toin Teien   45

Kyoto   46
Kamigamo Shrine   48
Shimogamo Shrine   50
Toji Temple   52
Kiyomizo   54
Ninnaji   56
Tenryuji   58
Kinkakuji   59
Ginkakuji   60

Ryoanji   60
Nishi Honganji   62
Shosei-en Garden   62
Nijo Castle   64
Ninomaru Garden   64
Enryakuji   66
Daigoji   68
Byodo-in   70
Ujigami Shrine   72
Saihoji   74

Nikko   76
Toshogu Shrine   78
Futarasan Shrine   79
Shinkyo Bridge   80
Taiyu-in at Rinnoji   82

Hiroshima   84
Hiroshima Peace Park   86
Origami   87
Itsukushima Shrine   88

Intangible Heritage   90
Bunraku   92
Kabuki   94
Kagura   96
Yuki Tsumuji Silk   96
Washoku   98
Gion Festival and Float Festivals   100
Bugaku   100
Washi Paper   102
Chakkirako   104

Kyogen	106	Katsuren Castle	148	**Shiretoko Peninsula**	**190**
Noh	107	Seifa Utaki	148	Shiretoko Five Lakes	192
Gagaku	108			Godzila Rock	195
		Hiraizumi	**150**	Brown Bears	195
Fuji	**110**	Motsuji Garden	152	**National Museum of Western Art**	**196**
Mount Fuji	112	Chusonji	154	**Ogasawara Islands**	**198**
Shiraito Falls	114	Kanjizaio-in Ato Garden	154	Minamijima Island	200
Fuji Five Lakes – Lake Ashi	115	Takkoku-no-Iwaya	156	Wildlife	202
Fujisan Hongu Sengen Taisha	116				
		Iwami Silver Mine	**158**	**Nagasaki**	**204**
Meiji Industrial Sites	**118**	Iwami Ginzan Silver Mine	160	Oura Cathedral	206
Kyu-Kagoshima Bosekisho Gishikan	120	Rakanji	162	Tabira Church	208
Shoko Shusielcan	122	Kigami Shrine	164	Egami Church	209
Nirayama Reverbaratory Furnace	124	Omori Townscape	164	Former Gorin Church	210
Glover Garden	124			Dozaki Church Bas-Relief	212
Hashima Island	126	**Individual Preserved Sites**	**166**		
		Mozu Tombs	168	**Tentative sites**	**214**
Kii Peninsula & Koyasan	**128**	**Himeji Castle**	**170**	**Hikone**	**216**
Kompon Daito	130	Kokoen Garden	172	Hikone Castle	216
Kongobuji	132	**Yakushima**	**174**	Genkyu-en	218
Banryutei	133	Shiretani Unsui Gorge	175	**Asuka**	**220**
Fire Ceremony at Ekoin	134	Yakusugi Land	176	Ishibutai Tumulus	220
Henro	135	Yaku Monkeys at Yakushima	178	Takamatsuzuka Tumulus	221
Okunoin	136	Kigensugi Cedar Tree	179	Kameishi Turtle Rock	222
Jizo at Okunion	138	**Okinoshima**	**180**	Tamatsu-zaka Murals	222
The Kumano Kodo	139	Okinoshima Miare Festival	182	**Kamakura**	**224**
Seigantoji Temple and Nachi Falls	140	**Shirakawa-go**	**184**	Tsruugaoka Hachimiangu Shrine	224
Nachi Taisha Shrine	141	Gassho-zukuri	184	Great Buddha of Kamakura	225
		Tomioka Silk Mill	**186**	Kenchojji	226
Okinawa	**142**	Shirakami Sanchi	188	Nagoe Kiridoshi Pass	226
Shuri Castle	144	Shirakami Beech Forest	188	Shomyoji	228
Shikena-en	146	Anmon-no-Taki Waterfall	189	**Notes**	**230**

Preface

One early spring afternoon this year, I walked out past the tunnels of fluttering cherry blossoms surrounding my two-room flat and took a bus towards the center of the city where I live, Nara. The capital of Japan through much of the 8th century, Nara is home nowadays to 350,000 people. But the very heart of the modern city consists of the largest municipal park in the entire country. Twelve hundred wild deer roam free around downtown, as they have done since a white deer was sighted carrying a god, it's said, over the hills in the year 763. I strolled along the busy main drag, and saw a stag waiting patiently for a green light. Not far away, two does were reclining near the front steps of our five-story glass-and-concrete City Hall, as if to remind passers-by of who rules the place.

Five minutes farther on, I found myself passing what was until recently the largest wooden building on the planet, the great 8th century temple called Todaiji. Inside stood the largest bronze sculpture in the world, a 53 foot-high Buddha. A fifteen-minute walk across the deer park would have brought me to the most sacred Shinto shrine in the land outside of Ise, known as Kasuga Taisha.

A ten-minute ride from the train-station would deposit me near the oldest wooden building on the globe, Horyuji, dating from the year 607. I saw the second highest pagoda in Japan poking above the trees and realized, yet again: After forty-four years of traveling the world almost without interruption – from North Korea to Easter Island and Ethiopia to Bhutan – I've never seen anywhere that feels or looks like Japan.

No wonder this book introduces you to wonders and traditions that you couldn't imagine finding anywhere else. Whenever I take a train to Kyoto, less than an hour from Nara, I'm greeted by a city that has given the world Zen gardens and geisha dances, 1000 year-old festivals and a Washoku cuisine that shifts with every tiny seasonal inflection. On a typical morning in the city, I visit Saihoji in the west, where there are 120 different kinds of moss, each glinting with a slightly different shade of green. From there it's a short taxi ride to Tenryuji, one of Kyoto's 1600 Buddhist temples, set beside a towering forest of magical bamboo, and serving up sumptuous traditional monks' lunches to visitors. And after a vegetarian feast, I head by cable-car up to Hieisan, in the northeast, a powerful, often snow-covered mountain where bells resound across slopes that once housed three thousand monastic buildings. I had been living in Western Japan for decades before I learned that the sacred heart of Hieisan, known as 'Enryakuji,' refers not to any single structure. The whole mountain is said to be a temple.

If I mention Japan to friends these days, I know they'll start talking about cutting-edge technologies and anime dramas, everything that goes with robots and wild fashions. It can be easy to forget, amidst all the sci-fi futurism of post-war Japan, that those minimalist devices that fit in the palm of your hand arise, in truth, from the same sensibility that once gave us haiku and pen-and-ink drawings made up mostly of empty space. And those machines that cry 'Welcome!' when you enter any shop are true to a Shinto spirit that sees a soul in every desk and blade of grass and, for that matter, bullet train.

Even after more than thirty years in Japan, therefore, I find myself surprised – and humbled – every hour. Whether it's the black-clad puppeteers staging propulsive dramas on a Bunraku stage in Osaka, forty-five minutes from my home, or the beautiful shrine of Itsukushima, lapped by water, just across from the haunting Peace Memorial in Hiroshima, each feels like an exercise in time-travel that can take me to several planets – and centuries – in a morning. At one point during my recent cherry-blossom walk, I looked up and realized that I was standing outside a building erected in the 8th century for storing all the Roman cups and Chinese carpets and Egyptian chests that arrived in Nara when it was the eastern terminus of the Silk Road.

'Don't you know?' said an Iranian gentleman, who'd taken up residence here because of the beauty and refinement all around. 'They call it the oldest museum in the world.' I didn't know. But every day brings me some fresh cultural inheritance I hadn't even guessed at. As I watched the deer, in a grove of wild plum trees, bowing to visitors from Shanghai and Paris – next to a 16th-century wooden structure once used for holding Buddhist texts, I thought: all of Nara, like all the other unforgettable sites you'll visit in this book, is at heart a treasure-hall, a family heirloom, for the entire world.

Pico Iyer
Nara, April 2018

World Heritage Map of Japan

Google map: www.bit.ly/WorldHeritageMap

QR code to go to Google Map

IWAMI

OKINOSHIMA

NAGASAKI

YAKUSHIMA

OKINAWA

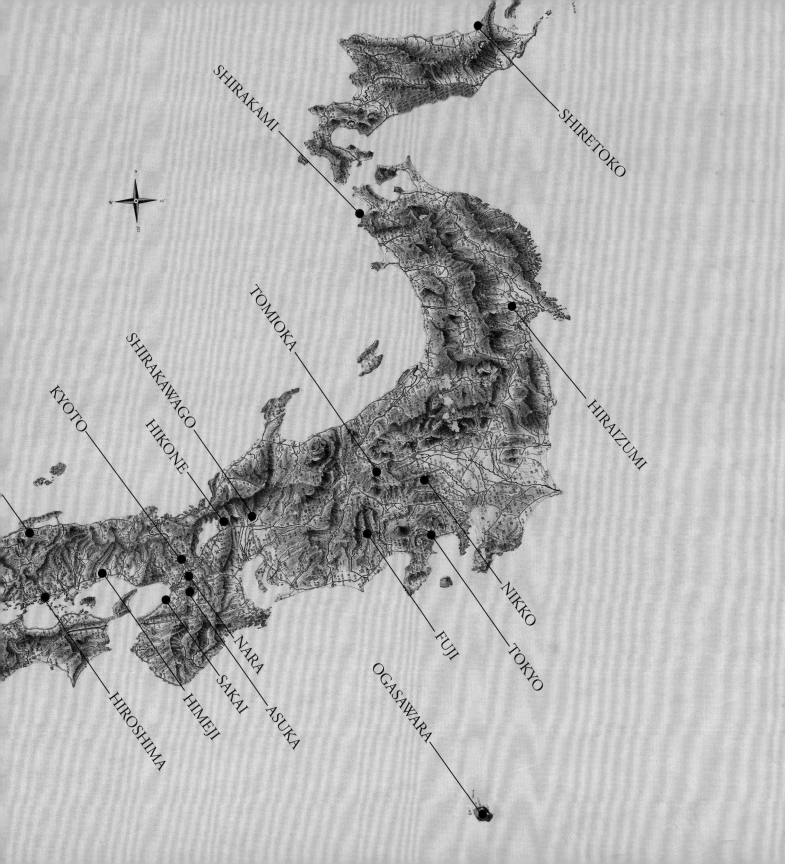

SHIRAKAMI

SHIRETOKO

TOMIOKA

SHIRAKAWAGO

HIKONE

HIRAIZUMI

KYOTO

NARA

NIKKO

FUJI

TOKYO

HIROSHIMA

HIMEJI

SAKAI

ASUKA

OGASAWARA

Introduction

Yoko Kawaguchi

Japan's Cultural World Heritage sites and Intangible Cultural Heritage cover nearly 1,500 years of human activity. They include Shinto shrines and Buddhist temples, castles and farmhouses, silver mines and factories, and the skeleton of a dome in Hiroshima which survived the atomic bomb. Also on the list are skills which have been honed through the centuries by the creative hands through which they have passed: paper-making, silk-weaving, music-making and dance, theatre and festivals, and the loving art of cooking and presenting food.

The buildings of Nara show how Japanese culture blossomed during the 7th and 8th centuries under stimuli from the Asian continent. The music of *gagaku*, to which the slow and stately dances of *bugaku* are performed, incorporates popular Chinese tunes from distant times. After the capital was moved to Kyoto in 794, Chinese influences were gradually assimilated into a radiant, distinctively Japanese style that flourished at the imperial court.

The refined culture cultivated by the aristocracy was in turn reshaped under the pressures exerted upon it by the inexorable rise of the samurai *(bushi)* class, in whose political grip Japan more or less remained from the 12th to the middle of the 19th century. Kyoto culture spread out across Japan, as powerful local bushi clans gained in confidence. But the *bushi* also had their own ethos and way of life, which seeped back into Kyoto society. Under their influence, much of what is familiar today in Japanese architecture emerged: floors laid with woven-reed *tatami* mats; sliding wooden-framed doors covered with *washi*, translucent white Japanese paper, that lets in a milky light. The early patronage of the *bushi* helped Zen schools of Buddhism take hold in Japan; the enthusiasm their leaders showed for collecting Chinese art, from ink-brush paintings to calligraphy and ceramics, had a profound influence on Japanese art and Japanese garden design, as well as on the development of the tea ceremony. On the one hand, there was the preference for what was austere, simple and pared-down – for paintings of shadowy outlines of distant mountains executed with brush and black ink, and gardens composed of raked gravel, stones and moss. Yet there was also the taste for opulent bursts of colour and for gold – for exuberant paintings of tigers frolicking

against a background of gold-leaf, and for cherry blossoms and majestic pines which seemed to burst forth from the screens upon which they had been depicted. The contrast seen in *noh* theatre between the performers' gorgeous brocade costumes and their stark masks and highly restrained, stylised movements encapsulates this duality. The rich artistic heritage which Kyoto jealously guards to this day illustrates the wide range of tastes shared by the country's warrior masters, yet underlying it all is the elegant aesthetic of the ancient courtly tradition.

Kyoto's political rival Tokyo, or Edo as the city was originally known, rose up in the 17th century along the brackish shores of Edo Bay. It became the seat of government after the warlord Tokugawa Ieyasu was appointed shogun in 1603. The dynasty he founded ruled Japan for the next two and a half centuries. This was a period of peace, which encouraged domestic trade and the development of the nascent industries which laid the groundwork for Japan's eventual emergence as a major manufacturing nation. In the cities, popular culture flourished among the common people, as prosperity filtered down from the merchant classes to among the artisans. Life could be difficult, but they went to the theatres, when they could afford it, to watch kabuki plays and *bunraku* puppet plays; they read books from lending libraries and bought *ukiyoe* (woodblock prints) of their favourite actors, of famous landscapes and of famous local beauties; they organised pilgrimages to climb Mt Fuji. The Shogunate ruthlessly proscribed Christianity, which had been introduced by Jesuit missionaries in the middle of the 16th century, but a trickle of trade (and information) continued to flow between Japan and the outside world through a tiny number of Chinese and Dutch merchants permitted to reside in tightly guarded quarters at Nagasaki.

Finally the Shogunate's creaking political and social structures were given a fatal blow by the appearance of a squadron of American battleships in Edo Bay in 1853. The question of how to deal with the threat posed by western powers, who were demanding that Japan should be opened up to trade with the rest of the world, threw into turmoil both the court of the shogun at Edo and the court of the emperor in Kyoto. The ultimate result was the end of the power of the samurai and the establishment of a new imperial government in 1868 in Tokyo, as Edo was now re-named. A new era was ushered in: the age of rapid westernisation. Western technology was eagerly embraced, and the trappings of western culture began to be adopted by the people, beginning in the cities. Railroads crisscrossed the country and factories sprang up. But Japan's mad rush to prove itself a contender on the world stage lead to the horrors of military expansionism and eventually the disasters of the Second World War. Atomic bombs were dropped on Hiroshima and Nagasaki in the weeks before Japan's surrender on 15 August, 1945. Japan's post-war occupation by Allied forces, led by the Americans, only ended in 1952. The resumption of diplomatic and cultural ties with France was symbolised by the opening in 1959 of the Le Corbusier-designed National Museum of Western Art in Tokyo. But Okinawa (the Ryuku Islands) remained under American control until 1972. After Okinawa's reunification with Japan, a painful, on-going examination has being taking place of the complicated relationship Okinawa, originally the Ryuku Kingdom, has had with the rest of the country. Shuri Castle, the

centuries-old bastion of the Ryuku kings, is a World Heritage site; its buildings burnt down in the last days of the war, but many of them have since been rebuilt.

Never have the Japanese forgotten that they are an island people. Japan consists of more than 6,800 mountainous islands, of which four (five including Okinawa, the chief island of the Ryuku Islands) are counted as the mainland. Nature has been bounteous: the Japanese archipelago, stretching from near Taiwan, with its subtropical climate, in the south to near Russia's Sakhalin Island in the north, is blessed with a rich variety of flora and fauna. Japan has four designated Natural World Heritage sites, apart from traditionally sacred places such as Mount Fuji and the Kumano Kodo pilgrimage route.

But nature is also frequently brutal: Japan is a chain of volcanic islands, buffeted annually by Pacific Ocean typhoons. When the Japanese walked through their dark towering forests of broad-leaf evergreens and conifers, when they waded into their rice paddies to plant rice seedlings, when they set out to fish on the open waves, they have always been aware of presences they called *kami*, translated inadequately into English as 'gods'. Various types of music and dance – from ancient courtly *gagaku*, to ritual performances of *kagura*, to the folk traditions of *chakkirako* – were, and continue to be, performed to honour, entertain and placate these *kami*. Buddhism dealt with the ultimate fate of the human soul, but meanwhile *kami* continued to preside over the natural world. Some of Japan's mountains are living *kami*; other *kami* descended upon ancient trees and boulders. Walk along the Kumano Kodo today or enter the Kasugayama Primeval Forest in Nara: the *kami* are still there.

The pairing of mountain and sea has been a constant motif in Japanese gardens since earliest times. Be it a small pond with a tiny islet just large enough for a single miniature pine tree – or even an area of raked gravel with a rock placed in it – this represents the vastest of oceans together with islands. Much has been written about asymmetry in Japanese gardens, but travel along Japan's winding, sinuous and hilly coastline and it begins to make sense. Come around the ridge of a mountain and suddenly a vista unfolds before you: jagged boulders and sea spray below; to one side, a smooth stretch of beach, perhaps, in a protected cove; on the other, promontories jutting out into the blue water in the middle distance; and then faintly, in the far-off haze, the outline of a conical mountain rising, seemingly, out of the sea. It is this variety which is captured in the design of Japanese gardens.

Gardens in Japan (and Japanese art generally) also frequently incorporate features which are only partially visible, that is to say, more suggested than actually seen. The Japanese have always appreciated things half-glimpsed – the suggestion of a presence: a waterfall, for example, veiled by the frond-like branches of a maple tree, recognised as much by the sound of the water and the smell of the damp earth, if not more so.

John Lander's photographs in this volume capture perfectly this half-glimpsed world of Japanese culture. Deeply knowledgeable himself, he yet refrains, as an artist, from spelling everything out. He makes you stop and ponder and use your own imagination. Afterwards, come to Japan and experience the country for yourself.

Foreword

'What is pertinent is the calmness of beauty, its sense of restraint.'
Kazuo Ishiguro

To adequately describe Japanese culture, architecture, history, customs and festivals would require volumes. I'd like to let the images tell the story insofar as possible. This book does not intend to be a guidebook nor an exhaustive encyclopedia of Japan's world heritage properties or intangible attributes. A handful of UNESCO sites have not been included, due to their inaccessibility or relative lack of impact on me personally. What has been included is the best of the best, in my view.

Intangible world heritage has been included as cultural entities such as kabuki perform-ances, noh theatre, Japanese cuisine, float festivals, ancient court music which add human elements to the mix. No matter how sublime a Japanese garden or unique the architecture of a temple may be, perfection can become sterile without traces of human activity.

Depending on readers' curiosity on the ori-gins that have shaped Japan over the course of one thousand years, a further reading list has been provided at the end of the book. Many sources are also available online.

For the sake of practical information, JNTO Japan National Travel Organization has long been the go-to place for reliable informa-tion. Clearly, some historical background is helpful so as to accurately put one's finger on the pulse of Japan and its heritage. The *Kojiki* or 'Record of Ancient Matters' was written in the 8th century for those truly eager to get at the heart of matters. The *Kojiki* is a collection of myths and songs concerning the origins of Japan which serves as the inspiration for many cultural practices in Japan that exist today.

Many Japanese words have entered the world's lexicon: *tatami, sushi, sayonara, ramen, cosplay* and *anime.* As interest in Japan and the numbers of visitors to the country have expanded, the list is growing. However, other vocabulary has not quite made it into colloquial talk as yet such as: *onsen, henro, jizo, karesansui,* et al.

A glossary of vocabulary used in the text and captions is provided at the end of the book. Use of Japanese words have been minimized as much as possible to avoid confusion.

John Lander
Kamakura, January 2019

NARA 奈良

Nara was once a thriving capital devoted to silk, higher learning and Buddhism. It was the seat of Japanese culture and power built against a backdrop of primeval forests. Part of its present-day allure is in the famous wild deer roaming around town, somehow setting the pace for the place. The deer inhabit the Kasuga Primeval Forest, come into town to beg for treats, then head back up to the hills come nightfall.

Japan's first official capital city was laid out, as Kyoto would be, on the grid pattern of Xian, China. This was not the only import from China. Besides *Kanji*, the writing system, Buddhism was introduced to Japan in Asuka and Nara. The Great Temple of Todaiji required two million laborers and 50,000 carpenters to build the place, housing the world's largest bronze statue the *Daibutsu* or Great Buddha – projecting an air of repose as it has for over a thousand years. Casting the Great Buddha drained Japan of almost all of its supply of gold and copper, nearly bankrupting the country.

The other icon of Nara is the five-story pagoda at Kofukuji Temple, hovering over Sarusawa Pond. It is hard to imagine that Kofukuji was once composed of 175 buildings, yet the temple complex still maintains an aura of sanctity and importance in its spacious grounds. Also within Nara's old town lies Gangoji, an ancient temple surrounded by stone *rakan* Buddha's disciples. Kasuga Shrine presents a unique spectacle with its moss-covered lanterns that punctuate the forest trails leading to the shrine while many bronze ones festoon the shrine compound itself. Kasuga Shrine holds an important place in the Shinto religion with ceremonies taking place here such as weddings and *shichi-go-san* for Japanese children kitted out in kimono to receive their blessings.

Further south lies Yakushiji and its intricately constructed pagoda. Nearby Horyuji and Hokkiji are linked together historically because of the similarity of their pagodas presumed to have been built by the same architect and builder. Further afield, Heijo Palace was rebuilt for Nara's 1300-year anniversary, along with the palace garden Toin Teien.

Kasuga-taisha Shrine 春日大社 was established by the powerful Fujiwara clan and rebuilt several times over the centuries. The legend is that the Fujiwaras invited a powerful deity to Nara, who arrived in town riding on the back of a deer. Consequently, wild deer from the forest above the city roam freely in its grounds. Kasuga is famous for its lanterns that have been donated by worshipers.

Hundreds of bronze lanterns hang from the buildings and hundreds more moss-covered stone lanterns line the approach to the shrine grounds. The Kasuga style of lantern is ornate and bears the images of the sacred deer. The lanterns, lit twice a year at the Lantern Festivals – Setsubon held in February and Obon held in August, light the way for ancestral spirits.

Kasugayama Primeval Forest 春日山原始林 has been untouched for thousands of years. It stretches across a large area behind Kasuga Taisha Shrine. Logging and hunting have been prohibited here since the year 841 and this has preserved the forest as a rare ecosystem with over 175 species of tree, rare birds and wild animals, including the sacred wild deer that roam around central Nara by day, returning to Kasuga Forest at night.

Todaiji 東大寺. Daibutsuden, the Great Buddha Hall Todaiji, shelters the world's largest bronze statue of Buddha: Daibutsu or Great Buddha. The Daibutsuden is the world's largest wooden building despite the fact that the reconstruction of 1692 is only two thirds of its original size. The casting of the bronze Great Buddha involved a huge proportion of the population and nearly bankrupted early Japan because of the enormous amounts of gold, wood and bronze needed. Today wild deer, regarded as messengers of the gods, roam the area.

Nigatsu-do at Todaiji 二月堂. Unfortunately, a fire broke out inside the hall in 1667 in the midst of a ceremony and the original building was destroyed and had to be reconstructed in 1669. The acoustics of the hall are said to be perfect with an inner sanctum, outer sanctum and worship hall that make it particularly well-suited for the rituals conducted here. It is also a popular sunset spot with many fine lanterns dangling from its eaves. Nigatsu-do is a National Treasure of Japan, and a part of Todaiji complex.

Kofukuji 興福寺 was once an important center for Buddhism in Japan. Since it was established by the Fujiwara clan who ruled Japan at the time, it also retained influence over the imperial government. One of the great temples of the Nara period, it features a five-story pagoda and many Buddhist art treasures. Today only a handful of the temple's 175 buildings remain standing, most of which date from the 15th century. Although its pagoda dominates the scene, octagonal halls contain most of Kofukuji's treasures, rarely open for viewing. The Octagonal Halls are noteworthy because of their unique architectural design and form part of the Western Japan Pilgrimage of 33 Temples.

Hokkiji 法起寺, or Temple of the Arising Dharma, was once known as Okamoto-dera. Completed in 638, it was founded by Prince Shotoku, who came to understand the Lotus Sutra here in a palace that was later turned into a temple. The small three-storied pagoda is the oldest in Japan. Though most of the other buildings at Hokkiji were destroyed by fire, this pagoda indicates what the rest of the temple would have originally looked like. The pagoda is similar to the one at nearby Horyuji, built by the same prince.

Horyuji Temple 法隆寺 was founded by Prince Shotoku in 607. The entire complex has been preserved making Horyuji a sort of museum of the building styles from the 7th century onwards. Enclosed by roofed corridors, the Western Precinct is home to the world's oldest surviving wooden structures built during the Asuka period and have never suffered damage or destruction. The Eastern Precinct showcases the octagonal Yumedono Hall of Dream Visions with its statue of Guze Kannon which was kept under wraps for centuries until 1884.

Gangoji 元興寺 was one of the great temples of the Heian period in Nara. Gangoji is comparatively more modest than its neighbors making it free of crowds who will be busy visiting the more famous spots in Nara. Nevertheless, it contains no less than three of Japan's National Treasures which include its main hall, simple as it may appear. Gangoji lies among narrow streets of the Naramachi district of old Nara. The temple's design has architectural influences from mainland Asia and many of the priests who first served here were from Korea and China. The grounds of Gangoji contain many ancient stone lanterns and grave markers, for which the temple is famous.

Yakushiji Temple 薬師寺 was constructed by Emperor Tenmu in the 7th century for the recovery of the emperor's sick wife. Yakushiji is one of Japan's oldest temples and is laid out on a central axis flanked by two pagodas. The main hall was rebuilt in the 1970s after being destroyed by fire and houses a Yakushi trinity, considered to be a masterpiece of Japanese Buddhist art. The

East Pagoda is the temple's only structure to have survived the many fires that have destroyed the temple repeatedly since the 8th century. It appears to have six stories, but there are really only three, in symmetry with the West Pagoda. The East Pagoda is considered to be a masterpiece of Japanese architecture.

Toshodaiji Temple 唐招提寺 was founded by Ganjin, a Chinese priest invited to Japan by the emperor to train priests and teach Buddhism. Consequently, its influence propagating Buddhism in Japan was monumental. Ganjin finally arrived in Japan after seven attempts to cross the South China Sea and eventually went blind. Toshodaiji's main hall was reopened in 2009 after restoration during which the building was dismantled and reconstructed. The temple's lecture hall was originally at the Nara Imperial Palace and was moved to Toshodaiji. Today, it is the only surviving building of the former palace. North of the temple, the tomb of Ganjin is surrounded by a moss garden.

Heijo Palace 平城宮. The design of the palace grounds was based on the Imperial Palace at Xian, China, which was contemporaneous with when Nara was capital of Japan from 710 until 784. Kyoto later became the capital and Nara's Imperial Palace was abandoned. The ravages of time and elements destroyed the buildings. Structures of the former palace complex have been reconstructed, including the Audience Hall Daigokuden, the largest building on the palace grounds. It was reconstructed for the occasion of the 1300-year anniversary of the founding of Nara as Capital.

East Palace Garden Toin Teien 東院庭園. This 8th-century pond garden was discovered by accident when workers preparing the ground for the rebuilding of the Palace found the remains of a stream garden that dates to the same period as the palace itself. The winding stream evokes the Chinese, Korean and early Japanese tradition of a banquet during which guests attempted to come up with original poems before cups of sake. All that remained at Toin Teien before reconstruction were the stream and the rocks placed along its banks. The style of Toin Teien anticipates aspects and elements of later Japanese garden designs.

KYOTO 京都

Kyoto has more World Heritage sites than any other place on Earth, though UNESCO lumps them all into one category: 'Historic Monuments of Kyoto'. Adding them all up, one by one, they number seventeen, not counting all the intangible heritage components. Tucked into cozy neighborhoods are thousands of temples and hundreds of shrines, plus the most awe-inspiring gardens in Japan. Kyoto was the capital of Japan for over 1000 years so it would be hard not to leave something of value behind. Because of the sheer numbers and significance of these treasures, it would be difficult to summarize the splendor of Kyoto's attractions in one written page. A select few are described below, which is not to say that the others are without note.

Ryoanji's garden teases the senses. A rectangle of furrowed sand suggests the rippling of waves on the ocean, with tiny moss-covered islands off center. Originally an aristocrat's country villa, Ryoanji is the most renowned of all dry landscape gardens. The carefully placed stones represent mountains, islands and even ideals. Ryoanji is composed of fifteen of these rocks on its sea of gravel. Not all of them can be seen at once, though it is said that if you can manage this you are on the cusp of enlightenment.

Repeatedly destroyed by fire over the centuries, Kiyomizu has been rebuilt on each occasion and is renowned for its imposing veranda supported by tall wooden columns and braces. Kiyomizu is one of the masterpieces of Japanese architecture, with such precise joinery that it was built entirely without nails. The temple's waterfall is counted among the ten purest water sites in Japan – drinking from this sacred well is said to bring good health and fortune. The ancient pond garden of Tenryuji, Temple of the Heavenly Dragon, is thought to have been designed in the 14th century by the renowned Buddhist monk gardener Muso Soseki. The composition here is of a large pond with stone islands, carefully laid out against the hillside for contrast in what is known as 'borrowed scenery'. Visiting a Japanese garden we ask ourselves what is deliberate, what is accidental. To enjoy the silence of a Kyoto garden is to appreciate the Japanese aesthetic, which puts value on what is implied not shown.

Saihoji is unique in Japan and the world through its presentation of 120 types of moss, that were used to create this ancient wonder. Bathed in a dreamy green light, the atmosphere is quiet and moist as the garden centers around a pond in the shape of the Chinese character for heart. The original temple structures vanished long ago, now only the moss garden and the sense of an ancient sacred place remains, and it is this that makes Saihoji so special. Kinkakuji Golden Pavilion was originally the private villa of a Shogun in the 14th century. The Golden Pavilion is composed of three types of architecture: the first floor is in the aristocratic residential style, the second floor is in the fashion of a samurai residence while the third floor is in Zen Buddhist temple style. The building is covered in gold leaf reflecting beautifully on the pond beside which it was built.

Kamigamo Shrine 上賀茂神社 is the oldest
Shinto shrine in Kyoto. Kamigamo Jinja has
preserved the legends relating to the birth
of its shrine deity, Wakeikazuchi. The Kamo
Shinto gods protect Kyoto from malign
forces. The area has many large oaks and
weeping cherry trees coexisting in harmony.
The austere conical sand mounds symbolize
purity. Kamigamo Shrine was under Imperial
patronage during the Heian period.

Shimogamo Shrine 下鴨神社 or Shimogamo jinja is an important Shinto sanctuary in Kyoto. The shrine occupies a 'power spot' at the confluence of two rivers. Shimogamo gives us the sense of being surrounded by nature as it sits within a forest, a remnant of a primeval forest mentioned in *The Tale of Genji*. The shrine is approached by a long trail through a forest of broadleaf trees. That is what makes this forest and shrine particularly special, considering that it is within a large city.

Toji Temple 東寺. Toji is a Buddhist temple of the Shingon sect in Kyoto founded by Kobo Daishi. Its name means East Temple. Toji's pagoda is the tallest wooden tower in Japan and has long been the icon of Kyoto. Though it was first built in the year 826, it has burned down four times and been rebuilt exactly as before each time. Toji, far more than merely a pagoda, is a huge 24-acre compound of temples and sub-temples and hosts a centuries-old antique market once a month in its huge domain.

Kiyomizu Temple 清水寺, or Kiyomizudera, is a major attraction in the city much celebrated for its awe-inspiring architecture. Not one nail was used in building the entire temple. The showpiece here is the 'dancing stage' veranda where performances were once held. Kiyomizu, meaning pure water in Japanese, takes its name from the waterfall in the hills nearby, the water itself being sacred.

Ninnaji 仁和寺 has always had strong imperial and aristocratic connections, as it was founded by Emperor Uda. Since the time of Uda the temple has been headed by an imperial prince, which endowed Ninnaji with many buildings and gardens in its spacious grounds. Among the buildings that have survived to the present day, are elegant palace-style buildings surrounded by Japanese gardens, temple halls, a massive entrance gate, belltower and tea houses. Its five-story pagoda dominates the entire scene. Ninnaji was the first imperial temple in Kyoto and is still active rather than a mere tourist attraction.

Tenryuji 天龍寺 has been ranked first among Kyoto's 'Five Great Zen Temples'. Muso Soseki, the temple's founding abbot and famous garden designer, is said to have created Tenryuji's garden which, unlike the temple buildings, survived several fires intact and is considered one of the oldest gardens of its kind. This is a *shakkei* or borrowed landscape garden, integrating the background scenery of the hills of Arashiyama as part of the garden's composition. Rather than physically entering the garden, it shows a 3D effect and was meant to be viewed from a distance. It is often cited as a one of the best examples of the use of borrowed scenery in gardens.

Kinkakuji 金閣寺, Temple of the Golden Pavilion, was built in 1393 as a retirement villa for Shogun Ashikaga Yoshimitsu. He intended to cover the entire exterior of the pavilion with gold, but only managed to coat the third floor with gold leaf before his death. Afterwards, his son converted the building into a Zen temple of the Rinzai sect named Rokuonji in accordance with Ashikaga's wishes. He also managed to cover the first and second stories in gold leaf as it stands today. This architectural treasure, reflecting in its surrounding pond, is a masterpiece of Japanese aesthetics.

Ginkakuji 銀閣寺 is a Zen temple at the foot of Higashiyama Eastern Mountain. The temple was formally known as Tozan Jishoji, built as a retirement villa for shogun Ashikaga Yoshimasa. Its formal name is Tozan Jishoji. The Silver Pavilion was modeled after Kinkakuji's Golden Pavilion. The legend is that there were originally plans to cover the pavilion in silver but this never happened. Even so the name Silver Pavilion stuck. The villa was converted into a Zen temple after Yoshimasa's death and is well known for its Zen garden, parts of which are more recent additions. The unique Kogetsudai Moon Viewing Pavilion adds an enigmatic element to the surrounding horizontal sea of gravel.

Ryoanji 龍安寺 rock garden is known as a dry garden or *karesansui* and is the most renowned of its kind in the world. The simple appearance of this Zen garden consists of nothing but stones and neatly raked gravel. The intention of the garden's design is obscure and up to each visitor's interpretation. Like a Zen *koan* puzzle, it is said that if you can see all of the 15 stones at once you will have reached enlightenment.

Nishi Honganji 西本願寺, Temple of the Original Vow, serves as the head temple of the Jodo Shinshu sect. Nishi Honganji is older than its neighbor Higashi Honganji and has more impressive architecture, particularly its intricate wooden gates. The Higurashimon Gate of Dusk is so elaborately and flamboyantly decorated that its name suggests that it should be viewed at dusk so as to avoid damaging the eyes. It is engraved with characters from moral tales and auspicious motifs.

Shosei-en Garden 渉成園 is a traditional Japanese formal garden thought to have been built in the 9th century on the site of Prince Minamoto Notoru's mansion. Fires in 1858 and 1864 burnt the walls and interior structures to the ground. They were restored, and in 1938 designated a National Historic Site. Within the grounds, there are several tea houses, a large pond, a small waterfall, stone lanterns and bridges. Shosei-en is part of the Honganji temples complex.

Nijo Castle 二条城, or Nijo-jo, was completed in 1603 as the residence of the first Tokugawa shogun of the Edo period. Even though the Tokugawa Shogunate moved its power base and capital to Edo Castle in Tokyo, they kept Nijo Palace in Kyoto as a reminder of who was in control. The entire castle grounds are surrounded by stone walls and moats. The palace survives in its original form with separate buildings which are connected by zigzag corridors with 'nightingale floors' that squeak when stepped upon as a security measure against intruders.

Ninomaru Garden 二の丸庭園 was refashioned by the renowned landscape architect and garden designer Kobori Enshu and is prominent in the grounds of Ninomaru Palace at Nijo Castle. The garden has a large pond with three islands and features carefully placed stones and pine trees. The garden is so very impressive that many visitors skip the tour of the palace itself just to enjoy its quiet beauty.

Enryakuji 延暦寺 is located on Mount Hiei hovering over Kyoto. It is the headquarters of the Tendai sect of Buddhism. Founded during the early Heian period, it was once one of the largest monasteries in the world. At its peak, Enryakuji had as many as 3000 sub-temples in its domain and a powerful army of warrior monks who engaged in power struggles with other monasteries and political leaders that eventually brought about its demise of power. Enryakuji is imbued with a solemn atmosphere as a place of training and as the home of the 'marathon monks'.

Enryakuji Marathon Monks 回峰行. Monks 'circling the mountain' is a tradition at Mounts Hiei and Enryakuji, going back to the practice of the warrior monks of old. Enryakuji has always been known for its esoteric and austere mountain practices. Devotion and selflessness are what's important in the Tendai Sect of Buddhism and it is thought that this can be achieved by circling the mountain on foot as the ultimate expression of devotion. These practices include a twelve-year course of circling Mount Heiei before dawn, and finally fasting for ten days without water or sleep. Very few monks have ever completed this goal in the temple's history, yet many still make the attempt.

Daigoji 醍醐寺. Within its grounds, Daigoji houses eighteen of Japan's national treasures. Among them are buildings belonging to Sanbo-in famous for the quality of its Japanese garden. The garden was laid out with a large pond, paths and bridges and is said to contain over 700 stones. Sanbo-in was designed for viewing from a specific perspective within the temple's buildings. Laid out in the Momoyama period (1573-1615), the garden's islands depict 'fortuitous crane', the 'tortoise' and the 'isle of eternal youth' – poetic terms that show stones and ponds can be poised in a prescribed, esoteric relationship.

Byodo-in 平等院 is well known in Japan, so much so that its outline is featured on the 10-yen coin. Byodo-in was originally a private residence like many Japanese temples. It was converted into a temple by the Fujiwara clan in 1052. The Phoenix Hall, the 8ft tall statue of Amida inside it and several other items at Byodoin have been declared Japanese National Treasures. The pond garden at Byodo-in is thought to be one of the best examples of a Pure Land garden in Japan.

Ujigami Shrine 宇治上神社. Although of modest appearance, Ujigami Jinja is thought to be the oldest shrine in Japan that is still standing and was once closely linked to Byodo-in Temple as its guardian shrine. The main hall is built in the *nagare-zukuri* architectural style. Pure water is important for a town like Uji, south of Kyoto, famous for its green tea plantations. Uji once had seven famous springs, though only the one at Ujigami still exists. Near Ujigami Shrine stands Uji Shrine and the two used to be considered as one and collectively known as Rikyukamisha until they were separated during the Meiji period.

Saihoji 西芳寺. The Moss Garden at Saihoji Temple is often called Koke-dera or Moss Temple. More than 120 different types of moss now grow at Saihoji, some developed naturally or even accidentally thanks to its nearness to the pond. Saihoji is one of the few temples in Kyoto where visitors must request an invitation in advance before their visit. Visitors are required to participate in tracing *sutras* before visiting the gardens. In this way the monks are able to maintain the integrity of the temple and garden and prevent mass tourism from destroying the tranquility of this unique retreat.

NIKKO 日光

The Japanese like to say 'never say you've had enough without having visiting Nikko'. Arriving at Nikko's antique railway station at first you find an undistinguished Japanese town with a long main street heading up a slope towards the surrounding mountains. There is no hint of the spectacle that lies in store just up the slope. The first clue that extraordinary sights await, is the gracefully arched Shinkyo Bridge spanning the rushing Daiya River below. It was here that a priest named Shodo crossed the torrents on the backs of two huge serpents. Afterwards a bridge was built to protect people from the dragons. Shinkyo Bridge is the gateway to Nikko's sacred sites.

For those who believe that Japanese style is always subtle and subdued, Toshogu shrine may seem a colourful contradiction. Shogun Ieyasu Tokugawa was the founder of a dynasty that ruled Japan for 250 years. He requested that on his death a modest grave be built at Nikko. Ieyasu's grandson, Iemitsu, had other ideas about modesty and what kind of burial was fitting for a shogun and began construction of a shrine which, to his mind, was worthy of his grandfather. 1500 builders, painters, sculptors and experts in lacquerware worked for two years to create Toshogu Shrine. Unlike the understated minimalism of most Japanese shrines and temples, here the artisans went for shock and awe, leaving no doubt about the wealth and power of the Tokugawa clan.

Intricate carvings of flowers and animals cover every surface, the most famous of which are three monkeys that 'hear no evil, speak no evil, and see no evil.' With millions of sheets of gold leaf standing out against the wood, Yomeimon Gate is the showpiece of the artisans' work with hundreds of bas-relief carvings. Later, a five-story pagoda was added nearby – its levels represent the five elements: earth, water, fire, wind and heaven, even though Shinto shrines do not normally have pagodas. Nearby Futarasan Shrine is more subdued, as is Rinnoji Temple and its serene pond garden.

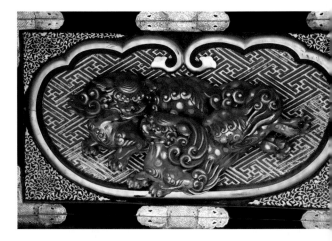

Toshogu Shrine 日光東照宮. Toshogu Shrines are found throughout Japan though the most famous by far is located in Nikko. The stable of the shrine's sacred horses bears a carving of the three wise monkeys who hear, speak and see no evil, a traditional symbol in Chinese and Japanese culture. Ieyasu's son, the second shogun Hidetada, ordered the construction of the Nikko Toshogu Shrine. Later, the third shogun Iemitsu had the shrine enlarged and lavishly decorated with gold leaf and coloured carvings.

Futarasan Shrine 二荒山神社. Futarasan Shrine is much older than its more lavish neighbor, Toshogu Shrine. It was founded in the year 782 by Shodo Shonin, the Buddhist monk who introduced Buddhism to Nikko and also established nearby Rinnoji Temple. This is an unusual juxtaposition of Shinto and Buddhism, particularly as they were both founded by a Buddhist monk – presumably to keep his options open. At the back of the shrine there is a spring of pure holy water, so pure that it is used for making sake.

Shinkyo Bridge 神橋. When the monk Shodo Shonin came to Nikko in order to tame the mountains, at first he could not cross over the Daiya river. Jinjaou, the God of Snakes, appeared from the clouds when Shoto burned a holy fire to ask for help. The Jinjaou threw two dragons into the river and these transformed themselves into the bridge. Shinkyo Bridge was lacquered vermilion in 1636, but was washed away by a flood in 1902 and rebuilt in 1904. It is considered to be the official gateway to Futarasan Shrine.

Taiyu-in at Rinnoji 大猷院廟 is the mauso-leum of Iemitsu Tokugawa, the shogun who was the grandson of Ieyasu. Rinnoji Temple was founded in the year 766 by the Buddhist hermit monk Shodo Shonin. It was once so important that it had 500 sub-temples under its rule. Rinnoji is best known for its Sanbutsudoh Three Buddha Hall and the gilded Taiyu-in mausoleum.

HIROSHIMA
広島

At 8.15am on 6 August 1945 the first atomic bomb in human history was dropped on Hiroshima. Even though Hiroshima's Industrial Promotion Building was almost directly underneath the explosion, it somehow avoided complete destruction.

However, the people who were inside at the time died instantly and the interior of the building was totally gutted. Its skeletal remains still stand today, desolate in the middle of Peace Park, to serve as a reminder to all of us of the hideous destruction that can be caused by an atomic bomb. The Peace Park Museum displays walls, otherwise white, stained with black rain, photos of victims' backs with imprints from their clothing seared into their skin, charred children's lunchboxes and other haunting reminders of this atrocity. The message is clear: never again.

On a far more peaceful note, not far from Hiroshima's city center, visitors take a ferry boat ride to the island of Miyajima, domain of Itsukushima Shrine. At the ferry landing, the visitor is greeted by the local inhabitants: wild deer which roam the village streets and the quay. After a short walk, the visitor sees the huge *torii* gate hovering in the sea as the watery gates to Itsukushima Shrine.

Looking back towards land, the shrine itself seems suspended over the water – a labyrinth of red lacquered pavilions sandwiched between the green forest behind and the ocean below. Inside and outside you wander down vast corridors. One hears the rustling of the trees overhead and the sloshing of the sea below. From a veranda the visitor again sees the *torii* out at sea from a different viewpoint, for Itsukushima opens directly onto the sea and is part of it, seeking not to overwhelm, but to charm by its very uniqueness.

Itsukushima is not merely a shrine or a view, it is an experience.

Hiroshima Peace Park 広島平和記念公園 is in the center of Hiroshima, dedicated to the city's legacy of being the first city in the world to suffer a nuclear attack which led to the death of 140,000 people. The Industrial Promotion Building is now known as the 'Atomic Bomb Dome'. The purpose of the Peace Memorial Park, the dome and its museum, is to not only commemorate the victims but also to preserve the memory of nuclear horrors and advocate world peace. The chilling and unforgettable displays in the museum show in vivid detail the catastrophe of nuclear war.

Origami 折り紙. Cranes at Hiroshima Peace Park. Origami is the Japanese word for paper-folding. This art has been handed down from parent to child through the generations. Origami normally involves the creation of shapes such as paper animals, the most common of which are cranes. The crane is a traditional symbol of longevity and good fortune, although they have also become a symbol of peace. This association between paper cranes and peace can be traced back to a young girl named Sadako Sasaki who died of leukemia ten years after the Hiroshima atomic bombing. Sadako folded cranes for eight months in hospital, until her death.

Itsukushima Shrine 厳島神社 on Miyajima Island was once thought to be so sacred that human beings were not permitted to live there. The shrine was built over water so that humans would not 'pollute' the sacred island. Today many ferries carry traffic between the island and Hiroshima, but because the island is still sacred, even now no trees may be cut for lumber, and the terminally ill are brought to the mainland to prevent death from occurring on the island.

INTANGIBLE HERITAGE
無形文化遺産

Cultural heritage does not end with monuments, temples or churches. It includes traditions and cultural attributes inherited from our ancestors. Culture is an expression of the ways of living developed by a community and passed on from generation to generation. It is what keeps us attached to our traditions and beliefs. This legacy includes artistic forms of expression. Customs refer to the common ways of living that are practiced by a society – in this case Japan.

The importance of intangible cultural heritage is not only the cultural manifestations but also the overall wealth of knowledge and skills that have been transmitted from one generation to the next. Intangible cultural heritage depends on those who can pass on their knowledge of traditions, skills and customs to the community and the next generation. This passing of the torch contributes to social cohesion, encouraging a sense of identity which helps individuals feel part of their community and society at large. Cultural heritage can take various forms, such as the performing arts: noh, kabuki and bugaku. It can be fun, taking the form of festivals such as float events in Kyoto and Hikone. Cultural heritage can take the form of rituals like *chakkirakko* or traditional arts and crafts such as *washoku* cuisine, *yuki tsumugi* silk or traditional *washi* paper.

Intangible cultural heritage is an important factor in maintaining cultural diversity in the face of increasing globalization. This encourages mutual respect for other ways of life which is so important in our modern world with its increasingly short attention span. There is no doubt that Japan is very wealthy in terms of its cultural heritage, from the grace and refinement of kabuki to the rough-hewn beauty of hand-made rice paper.

Bunraku 文楽 is a special type of Japanese puppetry that has developed over a period of twelve centuries. It has long been considered popular entertainment for ordinary people. *Bunraku* developed around stories based on the daily lives of merchants in Osaka. These vivid tales, full of the joys and sorrows of daily life, made the shows popular with local townsfolk. The puppet masters remain in full view, while their assistants, disguised in black clothing, lurk in the dark shadows and provide the extra element that makes the shows so intriguing.

Kabuki 歌舞伎 is a traditional Japanese form of theater rich in showmanship, involving elaborately designed costumes, dramatic wigs, meticulous makeup and exaggerated voices and movements, all performed exclusively by male actors. Highly-stylized gestures convey meaning to the audience. The plots are based on historical events, moral conflicts, love stories and tales of tragedy or conspiracy. The use of dynamic stage sets, incorporating revolving platforms and trap doors permit quick scene changes and the sudden appearance and disappearance of characters. These elements combine to produce a unique and stunning performance. Kabuki is recognized as one of Japan's three major classical performing arts along with noh and *bunraku*.

Kagura 神楽 literally 'entertainment of the gods' has its origins in Japanese mythology and predates kabuki and noh as performing arts in Japan. It was originally performed only by Shinto priests and acolytes during ceremonies to entertain Shinto divinities. The spectacle starts with a ritualistic dance to welcome the deities and is followed by entertaining performances. Performers dressed up in elaborate costumes dance to music from traditional Japanese instruments. The performers play deities, demons, and sometimes humans who appear in ancient Japanese mythology. Hayachine *kagura*, an austere form of *kagura* from the mountains of Iwate Prefecture, has been given intangible UNESCO status, although all forms of *kagura* share similar qualities.

Yuki Tsumugi Silk 結城紬 is a high-grade silk produced using folk techniques handed down since the 8th century. From the spinning to the actual weaving, all the work is done by hand and results in silk with a unique texture. The spinner produces thread of a uniform thickness based on whether it will be used as warp or woof. It is the only fabric in the world where the yarn is not reinforced by twisting. It is woven on types of looms which have been used for over a thousand years. Yuki is a fertile region along the Kinu River in Saitama Prefecture with a long history of sericulture and weaving using these techniques.

Washoku 和食 traditional Japanese cuisine has drawn attention from all over the world for being healthy, decorative and delicious. It is simultaneously simple yet complicated, plain yet sophisticated. Seasonal specialties play an important role in Japanese cuisine. Preparation involves maximizing natural flavors of the ingredients, while enhancing their beauty through artful presentation. The most accessible version of this cuisine for most Japanese is the New Year's feast.

The Gion Festival 祇園祭 is the grandfather of all the float festivals in Japan. The Gion Matsuri has a long history dating back to the year 869 when it was first staged as a purification ritual to appease the gods during outbreaks of epidemics. Even today, every July huge crowds flock to Kyoto for this annual event. However, this is not the only colorful festival involving elaborate and ornate floats in Japan. The Hikiyama festival held each April in nearby Nagahama hosts the additional attraction of kabuki performances acted by children, on tiny, intricate stages carried on the floats. Enormous community and group efforts go into these productions.

Bugaku 舞楽 is a traditional dance that has long been performed for Japanese imperial court audiences and the elite for more than twelve hundred years. After World War II, the dance, known for its slow and exact movements, began to be performed for the public and has even toured around the world. The dancers wear finely designed costumes which include elaborate helmets made of brilliantly decorated cloisonné. The music and dance pattern is repeated several times, giving it a somewhat monotonous quality. Some *bugaku* dances depict legendary battles, others enact encounters with divine characters or mythical beasts. When Buddhist culture came to Japan via Korea and China in the 7th century, it brought dance traditions along with it. *Bugaku* incorporates items from Buddhist culture and traditional Shinto elements. These influences eventually mixed together and over the centuries were refined into something uniquely Japanese.

Washi Paper 和紙. Traditional Japanese paper is made from plant fibres, the nature of which enables the absorption of inks and dyes. Since the fibres are positioned at random, there is no consistent grain to *washi*, which makes this type of paper resistant to creasing, tearing and wrinkling.

Traditionally-made Japanese *washi* paper is acid free and some examples remain in good condition after hundreds of years. For centuries, colorful designs applied by woodblock have been made for decorative use in screens, lamps and blinds, taking advantage of its translucency. The village of

Higashi Chichibu in Saitama Prefecture stretches along the banks of the Ogawa River, whose clear waters have been used for traditional paper-making in the region for centuries. Flower petals and different types of grasses are added to the basic pulp to create diverse colors, designs and textures.

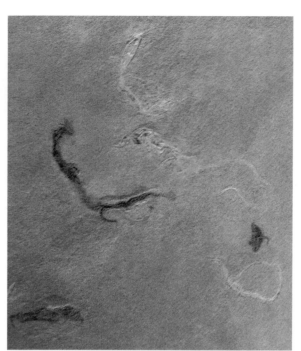

Chakkirako チャッキラコ is a folk dance that blesses the harvest and prosperity for the New Year for the townsfolk of Misaki, located at the tip of the Miura Peninsula. The *chakkirako* ritual is a traditional event held in this fishing port famous for its tuna markets. Girls aged 5 to 12 perform dances to music holding fans and bamboo sticks called *chakkirako*. There is no established theory behind the origin of the ritual, but it has been performed as a prayer for a good catch of fish since the Edo period.

Kyogen 狂言. *Kyogen* is a traditional form of Japanese comic theater, meaning literally 'wild speech'. It has close links to noh theater even though the contents of the two forms could not be more different. Movements are exaggerated with slapstick elements, making the play easy to understand for everyone. Few props or stage sets are used, and unlike noh theater, the actors do not wear masks. The emphasis of *kyogen* is on dialogue and action rather than music or dance. Short pieces are presented as a sort of intermission between noh play acts. Many elements in *kyogen* have influenced kabuki theater.

Noh 能. The word itself is derived from the Japanese word for 'skill' or 'talent' in which natural forces play an important role. To enjoy viewing a noh performance, the audience focuses on the theatrical costumes as well as the creeping movements, the stomping on the stage, the curious method of heel-and-toe walking. Fans and masks also play important roles. The slow tempo of noh takes the viewer back a few centuries to a time free from distractions – in effect stopping time. There is pleasure to be had in puzzling out the vague subtleties and discovering the richness of the associations. The language in noh defies translation even into modern Japanese. All in all, a noh production is an event unlike any other.

Gagaku 雅楽 literally means 'elegant music' and was originally performed exclusively at the Japanese imperial court for formal banquets and sacred rituals. Since *gagaku* had always been associated with the imperial court and was hardly ever heard by common people, it consequently remained static for centuries. Today it is also often performed during ceremonies at temples and shrines and also as accompaniment to *bugaku* dance performances. The instruments used are: *koto* or Japanese zither, *biwa* or Japanese lutes, flutes and traditional Japanese oboes, drums and mouth organs.

FUJI 富士

Long seen as an icon for Japan, Mount Fuji is more than just a volcanic mountain. It was the subject of Katsushika Hokusai's renowned series of woodblock prints: *36 Views of Mount Fuji*. It has been featured in countless novels, works of art, plays, songs, legends and poems. Consequently, UNESCO listed it as cultural heritage, rather than a natural site. The Japanese affectionately call the mountain Fuji-san, as if it were a person. Fuji does seem to be something of an enigma, invisible for days at a time then suddenly appearing – seemingly out of nowhere. Its nearly perfect symmetry can be seen from hundreds of kilometers away on a clear day.

Mount Fuji has always had something of the mystical and religious about it. The physical mystery of Fuji is that it changes its look, not only seasonally but daily. Fuji's majestic form and volcanic activity inspired awe and with it religious practices that linked nature with people, Shinto and Buddhism and became a center for ascetic religious practices.

Even today on the upper regions of the mountain there are pilgrim routes and shrines. Surrounding Fuji are a series of Sengen Jinja Shrines – all devoted to the peak. Despite its beauty, especially when it is capped with snow, people often forget that Fuji is still in fact a volcano that erupted three centuries ago. In spite of this sober truth, more than 300,000 people climb Mount Fuji every summer. An old Japanese saying goes: 'A wise man climbs Fuji once, but only a fool climbs it twice'. In other words, once is enough. Most people are content to view the spectacle from afar, ideally from one of the five surrounding lakes. Fuji Hakone National Park was established back in 1936 but has since expanded to include the Izu Peninsula and now encompasses three prefectures: Kanagawa, Shizuoka and Yamanashi in over 1200 square kilometers. All that space with Mount Fuji at the center, means there are plenty of attractions. These include waterfalls, Fuji Five Lakes, and Sengen Shrines.

Mount Fuji 富士, or Fuji-san as it is called in Japan, is the country's highest mountain at 3,776 meters in altitude. Mount Fuji is an active volcano that last erupted in 1707 killing hundreds of people and started fires as far away as Tokyo. By some accounts, Fuji is due for another eruption as its cycle appears to be every 300 years and it is classified as dormant but not extinct. Fuji straddles Shizuoka and Yamanashi prefectures just west of Tokyo from where it can be seen on a clear day. Mount Fuji's symmetrical cone is a well-known symbol of Japan and is frequently visible in works of art.

Shiraito Falls 白糸の滝 water source comes from Mount Fuji's melted snow which is considered to be sacred water. Its beauty is often compared to gentleness and feminine grace because the water falls in a more wispy fashion than the usual shock and awe thundering. It is part of the world heritage sites associated with Mount Fuji because of its connection with the mountain's water and snowmelt. It has also been designated as a Place of Scenic Beauty as well as a Natural Treasure of Japan.

Fuji Five Lakes – Lake Ashi 芦ノ湖, or Ashinoko Lake, is a scenic lake in the Fuji-Hakone area known for its views of Mount Fuji and its numerous hot springs. Two villages exist by its shores: Hakone Machi and Moto Hakone, from where there are excellent views of the lake and, if you are lucky, on a clear day a view of Mount Fuji from Moto Hakone. Of the Fuji Five Lakes, Ashi is one of the most accessible, but Lake Kawaguchi has incomparable views of the mountain and direct train access from Tokyo.

Fujisan Hongu Sengen Taisha 富士山本宮
浅間大社 is well known as the headquarters of
over 1,300 Sengen shrines across Japan. The
object of worship here is Mount Fuji – the
highest mountain in Japan and still believed
to be sacred. People venerate this shrine as a
guardian deity for disaster prevention,
navigation, fishing, agriculture and weaving.

MEIJI INDUSTRIAL SITES
明治日本の産業革命遺産

Japan's interest in industry began after the Meiji Restoration following many years of isolation from the rest of the world, caused by the Tokugawa Shogunate. The Meiji Emperor restored imperial rule over Japan, bringing in modernization and industrialization. This meant opening up Japan to the rest of the world after 220 years of reclusiveness. Following the end of the seclusion policy, the new Meiji government promoted industry as a national goal, which brought about industrialization. This was possible only by recruiting experts and advisors from Europe and America to oversee this rapid development. Meiji denotes enlightened rule and the goal was to combine modern advances with traditional Japanese values. Through industrialization, Japan was able to influence the country's economic and social prospects.

Japan's Meiji Industrial Revolution is relevant to world history as it demonstrates the rapid growth Japan went through in just 50 years. Certain industries were at the forefront: shipbuilding, steel works, railways and coal mining. Some of these sites now look almost quaint – reflecting Meiji period architecture and are not at all industrial-looking. Shoko

Shuseikan and its Japanese garden in Kagoshima are perfect examples of this. Likewise, the residences of European and American advisors such as the Kagoshima Spinning Engineers House where western engineers and advisors lived while working on nearby sites. Glover Garden was once the estate of Thomas Blake Glover, a Scottish trader with tremendous impact on the modernization and industrialization of Japan. His Nagasaki home and garden is anything but industrial. Besides Glover's main business enterprises with Mitsubishi and shipbuilding, he was also involved in setting up Kirin Brewery.

The most haunting and industrial-looking of these sites is Hashima Island, the former location of Mitsubishi coal mine. In 1810, coal was discovered on the island which was populated with coal-mining families from 1887 to 1970. When the mine closed down, the company moved everyone to mainland Nagasaki to new homes and jobs. The island is also called Gunkanjima or 'Battleship Island' which refers to its shape. Left to rot in the 1970s, it became a popular 'urban exploration' site for adventurers and daredevils despite the dangers involved. Today, safe, guided tours are available.

Kyu-Kagoshima Bosekisho Gishikan
旧鹿児島紡績所技師館, or Kagoshima Spinning Engineers House, is similar to its counterparts in other Japanese towns such as the foreigners' houses in Yokohama, Nagasaki or Kobe. These were known as Residences *Ijinkan* 'Foreigners Residence'. This classic Meiji-period building was constructed in 1866 to house British engineers and is one of the earliest Western-style buildings in Japan.

WORLD HERITAGE JAPAN 121

Shoko Shuseikan 尚古集成館. The end of the Edo period coincided with the appearance of ships from Western powers in Japanese waters thanks to Commodore Perry's black ships cruising into Tokyo Bay in 1853. Japan recognized that it faced an external threat and consequently Shimadzu Nariakira promoted modernization and industrialization projects on an increasingly larger scale. He did this by constructing an industrial complex near Kagoshima. Today, it is not a factory but the Shoko Shuseikan Museum.

Nirayama Reverberatory Furnace 韮山反射炉 was once an iron-smelting facility in Izu, Shizuoka. The furnace represents the beginnings of modern iron production in Japan. Nirayama Reverberatory Furnace represented the most advanced technology of the time. Iron produced there was cast into cannons.

Glover Garden 旧グラバー住宅 is a park in Nagasaki built for Thomas Blake Glover, a Scottish entrepreneur who contributed in a big way to the modernization of Japan. Within the gardens stand the Glover Residence, the oldest Western-style house surviving in Japan, as well as statues of Puccini and Chouchou-san of Madame Butterfly fame. Glover's home and surrounding gardens overlook Nagasaki Harbor.

Hashima Island 端島炭坑 was once populated by 5000 coal miners, but was abandoned in 1974. The island was left to the elements and now serves as a time capsule of the past. A cameo role in the 007 James Bond *Skyfall* movie put it back on the map. It is often called Gunkanjima or Battleship Island on account of its shape. Before the place became famous, it was slated to become a huge trash pit, but preservationists put a stop to that plan. Alighting from the boat onto the island is like entering a sci-fi scenario, with its crumbling and ruined concrete apartment buildings and collapsing stairways, twisted metal girders and plant life growing in the cracks. Access to many of the sites on the island is prohibited for safety reasons.

KII PENINSULA 紀伊半島
KOYASAN 高野山

Koyasan: It is 6am and the temple gongs are being rung, the only sound heard in the past eight hours. Clusters of monks assemble in the predawn light for their morning meditation. Unlike many famous temples in Japan that have become mere tourist attractions, Koyasan's temples carry on as monasteries. They house monks, pilgrims and visitors and conduct ceremonies as they have for a thousand years. The hilltop village's winding streets, temples, gardens, pilgrims, monks and special ambiance has a soothing effect on visitors. Many temples offer accommodation to pilgrims and other visitors. This helps support the temples financially and keeps the tradition of the Buddhist pilgrimage alive.

Linked to Koyasan is the Kumano Kodo. For over a thousand years, people from all levels of Japanese society have become

aristocrats. Later, towards the 15th century, commoners started going on these pilgrimages and the numbers of pilgrims increased dramatically. Koyasan, where Kobo Daishi's grave is located, is often considered the last stop of the Shikoku Pilgrimage as well as the Kumano Kodo Pilgrimage. Though there are countless small shinto shrines along the route, the most imposing site is Nachi Taisha with its thundering waterfall, the waters of which are considered to be purifying and perfect for cleansing the spirit.

The Kumano Kodo trails are all linked to each other. These pilgrim trails not only unite Koyasan and Kumano, but also mountain asceticism, Shinto and Buddhism. Shinto, the original animistic religion of Japan, and Buddhism have coexisted alongside each other for centuries. Consequently, it is not unusual to see Shinto shrines within

Kompon Daito 根本大塔 was begun by Kobo Daishi in the year 816 and was completed in 887. This massive structure represents the ideals of Shingon Esoteric Buddhism and is known as the Fundamental Great Stupa. The building was the first pagoda in Japan in the *tahoutou* style. Besides the numerous temples and monasteries at Koyasan, the main attractions of the village is the Great Stupa of Daito. Koyasan is the headquarters of Shingon Esoteric Buddhism founded by Kobo Daishi.

Kongobuji 金剛峯寺. Temple of the Diamond Mountain Peak, the head temple of Shingon Esoteric Buddhism in Japan, was founded by warlord Toyotomi Hideyoshi to commemorate the death of his mother. Besides its famous dry landscape garden and its association with Kobo Daishi (774-835), the temple is renowned for its artwork displaying the life of this famous monk, poet and artist who was one of the leading figures in Japanese history.

Banryutei 蟠龍庭 rock garden is Japan's largest dry landscape garden with 140 granite stones arranged to suggest dragons emerging from clouds to protect the temple. The garden is to be found within the grounds of Kongobuji Temple. The stones were brought in from Shikoku, the birthplace of Kobo Daishi in homage to him. The garden's size and magnificence rivals that of many other dry landscape gardens found throughout Japan.

Fire Ceremony at Ekoin 恵光院, a temple with accommodation facilities called *shukubo* for pilgrims and visitors. Such temples encourage guests to experience Japanese customs and culture. Koyasan is one of the best places to experience a temple stay in Japan as it invites visitors to witness morning prayer services and fire-burning ceremonies.

Henro 遍路 is the Japanese word for pilgrim. They are recognizable by their white clothing, sedge hats and special walking sticks with bells. Koyasan is linked to the Kii Kumano Kodo pilgrimage trails and the followers of Kobo Daishi who is buried there. There are said to be some 100,000 pilgrims each year who take on the challenge of the 88 Shikoku Pilgrimage. The traditional route begins at Ryozenji near Tokushima and ends at Koyasan as the final stop.

Okunoin 奥の院 is the cemetery where Kobo Daishi – the founder of Shingon Buddhism and one of the most revered persons in the history of Japan, rests in eternal meditation. Okunoin is over 1200 years old and is considered to be one of the most sacred places in Japan and is surrounded by Japan's largest graveyard. People from all over the country, lie buried here, including former feudal lords, politicians and many other prominent personalities. The extraordinary central mound is created by tier upon tier of thousands of Jizo figures.

Jizo at Okunoin. Many Jizo statues, representing the bodhisattva Jizo Bosatsu, are found all around Japan but especially here at Okunoin Cemetery in Koyasan, as they are guiding spirits of the dead. They are usually shown in the form of a monk with shaved head with a red hat or bib. Jizo are also guardians of travelers, so pilgrims will often tidy up the statues or put on new bibs or hats as a form of veneration. Red bibs are especially common as Jizo are believed to be the guardian spirits for children.

The Kumano Kodo 熊野古道 is a network of pilgrimage routes, trekked for centuries by the Japanese from all levels of society. Kumano has been sacred since prehistoric times, associated with animism in which mountains and water are key elements in shaping the Japanese sense of spirituality. Kumano is considered to be the abode of the gods by the Japanese. Along the Kumano Kodo pilgrims walk through leafy paths deep into the mountains every year to purify themselves, praying to deities dwelling in the trees and rocks. Over time, hiking the Kumano Kodo became less of an animistic or Shinto rite, especially after followers of Kobo Daishi made it into a Shingon Buddhist pilgrimage route. Koyasan is considered to be a major stop before or after the Shikoku Pilgrimage Trail. In modern times, tourists have largely replaced pilgrims.

Seigantoji Temple and Nachi Falls 那智滝
The Temple of the Blue Waves was built
next to Nachi Waterfall – a site of nature
worship. Seigantoji is an important part of
the Kumano Sanzan complex and the first
stop along the Kumano Pilgrimage Trail,
although these days those who follow the
hiking trails are not so apt to follow the
exact order of the stops along the way. Nachi
Falls is the largest in Japan at 436 metres.

Nachi Taisha Shrine 熊野那智大社. The
Kumano Kodo route connects this shrine to
Hongu Taisha Shrine, Hayatama Taisha
Shrine and Koyasan. Even today Japanese
pilgrims trek these routes, visiting these
historically important shrines and temples.
Serious *henro* travel to all three sites to
complete their pilgrimage. Kumano Nachi
Taisha is surrounded by cedar forests, has a
sacred camphor tree and is located next to
Nachi Waterfall and Seigantoji Temple
Pagoda. Nachi Shrine is also a part of the
Western Japan 33 Temple Pilgrimage Route.

OKINAWA 沖縄

When people think of Okinawa, images of white sandy beaches usually come to mind – a kind of Japanese Hawaii with a relaxed, tropical atmosphere. Its language, culture, cuisine and temperament are very distinct from mainland Japan. Okinawa has had a turbulent history especially considering that it only became a part of Japan a couple of hundred years ago. Dig a little deeper and treasures are to be found.

From 1429 to 1879 Okinawa was an independent country known as the Ryukyu Kingdom, which was at the nexus of East Asian trading routes. Okinawa's heyday was during the Gusuku period in the 12th century, when the Kingdom of Ryukyu Islands was at its peak. During this time, certain chieftains established themselves as regional kings. It was in 1879 that Okinawa became part of Japan after the Meiji Restoration and the islands became the Okinawa Prefecture. King Shotai at Shuri Castle was deposed, moved to Tokyo and made a marquis in the Meiji system of peers.

Gusuku refers to castles or forts with thick stone walls composed of limestone or corals. One of the notable things about these *Gusuku* fortress walls is that they follow the contours of the land. There are several *Gusuku* ruins in Okinawa: Katsuren, Zakimi, Nakagusuku and Nakijin. Some of them have been partially reconstructed with their walls reinforced. These sites are found on windswept hilltops with sweeping views over the terrain as protection from neighbors. None of the original castles or palaces survive.

During the time of the Ryukyu Kingdom, certain sites became designated as sacred grounds such as Seifa Utaki. There are several of these sites around Okinawa, though Seifa Utaki is the best preserved, having been recognized as a sacred place since the earliest period of Ryukyu history. For Okinawans it is significant – this is where Amamikyu, the Goddess of Creation first arrived in Okinawa. None of the buildings at Seifa Utaki survive; only sacred caves and nature trails remain.

Shuri Castle 首里城 served as the center of the Ryukyu Kingdom and its politics, foreign affairs and culture. With architectural influences from China and Japan, the castle retains exceptional cultural and historical merit for its unique stonework and architectural design. It was almost totally destroyed during World War II, but was reconstructed in 1992 on its original site, based on historical records and photographs. Although the current castle is a reconstruction, the replica is meticulously faithful to the original. Its architecture is a reminder of its geopolitical role in the past.

Shikina-en 識名園. Connected to Shuri Castle is the unique Shikina-en Garden which combines elements of Japanese, Chinese and Okinawan influences. It was built at the end of the 18th century as a second home for the royal family of the Ryukyus and to entertain VIP guests. Its restoration took more than 20 years. The garden's focal point is a hexagonal pavilion. Designed as a strolling garden, it is meant to be walked around rather than viewed from one particular angle.

Katsuren Castle 勝連城 was built in a style that places four flat terraces along an uphill slope. The castle walls were built taking into account the terrain, employing walls snaking upwards into the contours of the hills on which they were built. Katsuren was the seat of Lord Amawari – a sickly child who had been abandoned in the mountains and left to die. However, he survived that ordeal and grew up to be a powerful leader, defeating an oppressive lord and taking control of Katsuren Castle. As there was no water, Amawari had many wells sunk within the castle grounds. Katsuren is the oldest and best preserved of all the castle ruins in Okinawa.

Seifa Utaki 斎場御嶽 was once the highest-ranking sacred place in the Ryukyu Kingdom. Forest and bare rocks were admired as objects presented as God made them and were celebrated in rites mixing animism with ancestor worship in a uniquely Okinawan form. Men were once prohibited, and even kings were supposed to dress as women before entering. It is considered to be one of the seven sacred places built by Amamikiyo, the god for ancient spirits of the Ryukyu people. Its deity is Ikoe-no-Okimi the highest goddess. The forest around Seifa Utaki was undamaged during World War II and is full of rare ferns, trees and orchids. Even today people worship at Seifa Utaki which is still regarded as a sacred site.

HIRAIZUMI 平泉

During the 12th century the Fujiwara family was the most powerful clan in Japan. Hiraizumi was chosen as the seat of power in the north of Japan. The town grew in sophistication and came to rival Kyoto, so much so that Hiraizumi was known as 'the northern capital'. However, Hiraizumi was razed in 1189 by Minamoto Yoritomo, who would soon become Japan's first shogun. The haiku master Matsuo Basho spoke of Hiraizumi after its demise in a famous poem: 'Summer grass - all that remains of ancient warriors' dreams'. The city never recovered its prominence, but it retains the Tohoku region's most precious historic and cultural properties. Thus, Hiraizumi still resonates with reminders of its illustrious past with over three thousand national treasures and its handful of historical sites.

The original Motsuji Temple no longer stands except for a modest replica – all that is left is its Pure Land Garden – one of the few to remain intact in Japan. The garden surrounding Oizumi-ga-Ike Pond reminds us of the artistic achievements attained during Hiraizumi's days of glory. The other main attractions are Chusonji Temple that was once made up of dozens of sub-temples, though only two remain. Konjikido Golden Hall is Chuson-ji's jewel in the crown and is dedicated to Amida Nyorai, the Buddha of Infinite Light. The hall is covered with gold leaf inside and out. The interior is decorated with shell inlay, intricate metal filings and gold and silver inlays over lacquer.

Kanjizaio-in Ato Pond Garden was commissioned by the wife of Motohira, the second lord of the Fujisawa clan. The temples burned down, but the Pure Land Garden and Dancing Crane Pond were restored to their original glory. Takkoku-no-Iwaya Bishamondo is a cave temple dedicated to the god of war but repurposed as a place to pray for peace. The site was originally a prison, then a Shinto shrine, then finally became a Pure Land Buddhist temple in the 12th century. The surviving Bishamon statues are still kept at the temple under wraps, only revealed to the public once every 33 years.

Motsuji Garden 毛越寺. This pond garden at Motsuji reflects 12th-century ideas about garden design as described in the *Sakuteiki*, Japan's oldest manual on gardens. The manual explains how elements such as beaches, rocky coastlines, bridges, mountains, streams and stones protruding from the lake's surface should be used in the composition of a garden. The beauty of the Oizumi-ga-Ike pond has remained unchanged for eight centuries, blending into the surrounding nature and the whole is one of the few remaining Pure Land gardens that have survived in Japan. The gardens were designed to recreate the concept of Buddhist paradise. Spirituality was built into the very foundations, designed to elevate the mind as well as entertain the eye. Motsuji is considered to be one of the pinnacles of Japanese garden design and unique in its austere perfection.

Chusonji 中尊寺 was built in 1124 and is one of the only two 12th-century structures at Hiraizumi to survive in original form. The other building that remains from the period of prosperity under the Fujiwara is the Kyozo Hall, which served as a repository for *sutra* (Buddhist scripture). While not nearly as impressive as the gilded Konjikido, it nonetheless predates that building by 16 years.

Kanjizaio-in Ato Garden 無量光院跡 is another excellent example of a Pure Land garden. Maizuru-ga-Ike Dancing Crane Pond is all that is left of the once great temple complex, yet Kanjizaio-in Ato remains as beautiful as it was when it was built in the 12th century. The garden has a large pond with curving coastlines, an essential aspect in Pure Land gardens. In the center of the pond lies an island – the focal point of the garden. Kanjizaio-in Ato is also a nationally designated Place of Scenic Beauty and was restored in 1978.

Takkoku-no-Iwaya 達谷窟 was built into the rock wall of a cliff 1200 years ago during the Heian period. The original Takkoku-no-Iwaya Bishamon Temple burned down and today its original form is unknown. The current building was constructed in 1961 and modeled after Kiyomizu in Kyoto. Takkoku-no-Iwaya was dedicated to the god of warriors in the 9th century during the Japanese expansion northwards and battles with the indigenous Emishi people. Officially, Takkoku-no-Iwaya is still on UNESCO's 'tentative list' as an addition to Hiraizumi sites.

IWAMI SILVER MINE 石見銀山

灰吹
Cupellation

Back in the 1500s a merchant visiting Shimane Prefecture noticed a glow up in the hills around Iwami. That glowing sparkle was found to be silver and work soon began to mine the precious metal. Iwami Ginzan became the largest silver mine in Japanese history and was active for four hundred years until it closed in 1923. The silver mines made a large impact on the neighboring villages which are part of its cultural landscape and make up important components of Iwami's world heritage status.

Work in these mines was tough with only chisels, hammers and candles for light. Conditions were harsh with back-breaking loads and poor ventilation, so few miners lived past the age of 30. The silver was transported on horseback to the nearby ports and loaded onto boats for distribution around the world. In its heyday, the mine produced one third of the world's entire silver production. Silver was widely used as currency at the time and silver from Iwami Ginzan was considered the ultimate in quality which gave it a high value. When the mine's silver production started to dwindle, copper and other minerals were mined instead. There are 600 pits and mine shafts within the Iwami Ginzan complex, though only a few may be visited due to safety concerns. The shafts most visited are Kamaya Mabu Shaft and Ryugen-ji Mabu Mine Tunnel.

Although the mine's neighboring villages such as Omori and Yonotsu are now sleepy villages, this was once a wealthy area with a lively mercantile culture. It was known to its trading partners on maps as 'The Silver Mining Kingdom'. Iwami Ginzan had a profound influence on neighboring towns and villages with regards to architecture, shipping and transportation routes. Most of these elements of its cultural landscape can be found in the village of Omori near the actual mines and in Yunotsu where products were stored and shipped from its quays.

Iwami Ginzan Silver Mine 石見銀山 was an active mine from the 16th through the early 20th century. The fine quality of the silver produced here had a huge influence on the local economy as well as on economies around the world. The remnants of this mining town and its old-fashioned shops hark back to the time when the town's prosperity was built on silver. These days Iwami Ginzan riches derive from tourism.

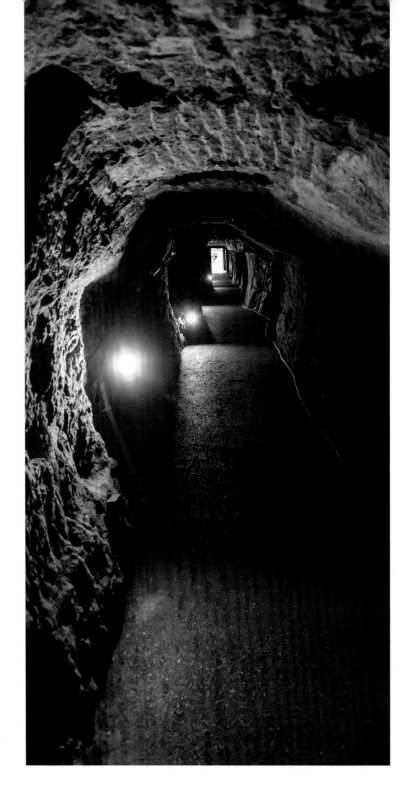

Rakanji 羅漢寺 is a Shingon Buddhist temple
built in 1776 to hold memorial services
for local silver miners. There are about
500 Jizo statues in the temple's caves, all
with different facial expressions. The Jizo
are well preserved thanks to the caves. They
were placed here to commemorate those
who died while mining silver, that they may
rest in peace. The technique for building
the arched stone bridges leading to the
temple was brought to Japan from China.

Kigami Shrine 城上神社 has been the guardian of Omori town for more than 400 years. On its ceiling are dragon frescos and locals believe that the dragon will howl if you clap your hands. The god of Kigami shrine is known as Okuninushi-no-mikoto – god of marriage, among other things. This Shinto god will help singles find the perfect partner and later bless their union. There are heart-shaped wooden votive plaques throughout the shrine compound covered with good wishes from hopeful couples.

Omori Townscape 大森町. The town of Omori flourished as the base for the Iwami Ginzan Silver Mine. Omori has antique homes from the Edo period, most notably that of the Kumagai family, wealthy merchants of the time. Kumagai House is richly decorated with ornate decor and furnishings, serving as a reminder of the town's former grandeur. Other historical buildings retain the architectural style and atmosphere of the time, with shops and cafes in renovated Japanese style. A handful of these merchant houses are open to the public as museums.

INDIVIDUAL SITES
個別サイト

Japan has many unique world heritage sites that are not always part of a larger collection, either as a city like Kyoto or a concept such as intangible culture or the Meiji industrial period. Each venue is special in its own way. Ogasawara is a pristine collection of islands far from the main islands of Japan, which thus far has avoided development, over-population and mass tourism, thereby keeping its environment intact. In a similar vein, the sacred island of Okinoshima has long been off limits to visitors and is strictly reserved for Shinto priests to visit the shrine there. Those who are allowed on the island are forbidden from speaking about it and taking even a single blade of grass from the place. Fishermen and all boats steer well clear of the place, viewable only from a distance. All this has preserved the island's purity and integrity. Yakushima is another remote island that has protected its environment of ancient cedar forests and untouched wildnerness.

Islands such as Yakushima and Ogasawara have had an easier time of preserving their environments, thanks to their remoteness but they are not the only nature spots with untainted nature. Thanks to the geography of Japan, certain remote places on the main island of Japan and Hokkaido have also maintained their integrity. Shiretoko Peninsula in Hokkaido is known for its pristine nature, brown bears, ice floes and rare sea eagles. Shirekami Sanso was the first nature spot in Japan to be declared a UNESCO World Heritage site, due to its rare beech forests.

These natural treasures are by no means the only individual places to have the World Heritage moniker. Himeji Castle is well known as the most elegant of all Japanese castles, despite its daunting position.

Shirakawago is famous for its unique architecture of a very different sort, where the small houses have steep, thatched roofs to protect them from heavy snowfall. Another architectural gem that has recently been included by UNESCO is the Museum of Western Art designed by Le Corbusier in Tokyo as part of a collective of Corbusier modernist architecture around the world. Also recently added is the Tomiola Silk Mill, built as part of the modernization and industrialization of Japan during the Meiji period.

MOZU KOFUN TOMBS
百舌鳥古墳群

The Mozu tomb complex originally consisted of more than 100 tombs, but today only half of these keyhole, round and rectangular tombs remain. It is commonly accepted that this tomb was built for the late Emperor Nintoku and the Imperial Household Agency of Japan treats it as such. Ancient iron items were placed in the tombs, such as arrowheads and swords, hoe and spade tips, and many more. Also found are gilded bronze antiquities such as horse tack and sash buckles. The tomb is off limits and protected by the Imperial Household Agency. The moats are a sanctuary for fish and waterbirds. UNESCO has officially inscribed the site as: Mozu-Furuichi Kofun Group: Mounded Tombs of Ancient Japan.

Emperor Nintoku 仁徳天皇. No firm dates can be assigned to Emperor Nintoku's life or reign, though he is considered to have reigned from 313 to 399 and is referred to by historians as a "Legendary Emperor". Daisen Kofun in the Mozu Tomb Complex in Sakai Osaka is considered to be his final resting place.

HIMEJI CASTLE
姫路城

Himeji-jo, begun in 1333 and remodelled in the 16th century, is just what a castle should be: imposing, impenetrable and beautiful. Designed to impress and inspire fear, it fulfills that function admirably, frowning down on the surrounding area from its perch up on a bluff. It stands prim, secure and foreboding, flaunting its power and showing off its style. Its formidable size is hard to perceive, as it was built on a distant hilltop. Unlike many other Japanese castles, it has never been destroyed by war, earthquake or fire and survives intact to this day though it has been renovated and repaired over the years. The maze-like interior was designed to confuse intruders, if not modern tourists.

Today Himeji Castle hosts regular art events as well as sound and light shows. Himeji-jo has made cameo appearances in several movies, including the 007 *You Only Live Twice* and Kurosawa's classic samurai movie *Ran*. The castle's halls, large airy rooms, cubbyholes and cozy chambers make ideal spaces for art exhibitions, though clearly that is not what the original designer had in mind.

As if that were not enough, at the castle's base, below the ramparts, there is an expansive series of Japanese gardens. Kokoen gardens were built on the former site of the feudal lord's west residence and are a series of gardens, each designed in a distinct style using different techniques and materials. Although Kokoen is a recent addition, no visit to Himeji Castle is complete without a stroll through its gardens.

Kokoen Garden 好古園. This series of gardens was designed by a team of Japan's top landscape architects and garden designers. It consists of nine separate gardens designed in various styles of the Edo period. Among the most noteworthy, are the lord's residence garden which features a pond with a waterfall, a tea garden with its requisite tea ceremony house, a pine tree garden, a bamboo garden and a flower garden. Overall the gardens were designed to be seasonally attractive and are relatively modern when compared to those found in Kyoto or Nara.

YAKUSHIMA
屋久島

Yakushima is best known for its mossy forests and ancient Japanese cedars that live longer and grow larger than those on the mainland. The weather is perpetually damp. Over the crest of every hill lies a valley and in every valley there is the play of shadows, damp air and the trickle of water that nourishes this moss-covered domain. Moss forms thick spongy spaces covering rocks, fallen logs and living trees, while hanging mosses cover the branches overhead. This world is green and full of life. Moss is a key element in bonsai and Japanese gardens and in this nation of moss lovers, Yakushima holds a special place of veneration with well over 600 species – one third of all the species in Japan.

It rains for over half of the year in Yakushima – more than anywhere else in Japan. Its isolation off the coast of Kyushu, has allowed the island to develop over the centuries into one of Japan's natural wonders. Some of the cedar trees here are thousands of years old. Noteworthy trees have nicknames like *Arch Cedar, Mother & Child,* and *Goddess & Twins.* Wildlife abounds including deer and monkeys. Like other remote places such as Ogasawara, Shiretoko and the Galapagos, these are not only beauty spots, but preserved spaces where precious plants and animals thrive as they have done for millions of years.

Visitors are reminded of scenes from the film *Princess Mononoke,* where lush, green, moss-covered rocks and magnificent cedars set the scene in that classic movie. The animator Hayao Miyazaki was so fascinated by the forests along the Shiretani Unsui Gorge on Yakushima that he spent time here sketching the scenery for his film. The mossiest of the ravines is even signposted as *Princess Mononoke's Forest.*

Shiretani Unsui Gorge 白谷雲水峡 is a
lush nature park containing a number
of Yakushima's ancient cedars such as
the Nidaio-sugi, Kuguri-sugi and Yayoi-
sugi. Shiratani Unsu Gorge is a popular
destination to see these forests without
much strenuous hiking with a network
of well-maintained trails that run along
the ravine. One of the main attractions
here is an area of the forest that served
as the inspiration for the film *Princess
Mononoke.*

Yakusugi Land 屋久杉ランド. In spite of its theme-park name, Yakusugi Land is actually a cedar grove where visitors can enjoy observing ancient trees and the epiphytes growing on them. This hiking trail here is quite flat and is suitable for beginners. There is a range of routes from 30 to 150 minutes long depending on weather conditions, hikers' ability and stamina. Several of the trees are more than 3000 years old, covered with epiphytes and other significant plants include *Sorbus commixta, Chamaecyparis obtusa, Ilex crenata, Rhododendron* and *Illicium arisatum.*

Yaku Monkeys at Yakushima ヤクシマザル. This particular species of macaque monkey known as a *yaku* monkey, is found only on Yakushima Island south of Kagoshima. Its natural habitat is found in the hills near UNESCO World Heritage protected lands. Today the forests have recovered after past logging and now enjoy the protection of being a national park, while other areas are World Heritage Sites. Most visitors come here to hike through the forests and admire the ancient cedar trees.

Kigensugi Cedar Tree 紀元杉 is estimated to be at least 3000 years old, one of the most ancient trees on Yakushima. Its age is made dramatically apparent via the gnarled bark, the great height and the enormous girth which give the tree a majestic presence. A wide array of living things have attached themselves to the tree, among them: Japanese cypress (*Chamaecyparis obtusa*), Rhododendrons, Japanese rowan (*Sorbus commixta*), Japanese holly (*Ilex crenata*) and Japanese star anise (*Illicium anisatum*). A visit to Kigensugi is an escape into primeval nature.

OKINOSHIMA
沖ノ島

For hundreds of years, Okinoshima has been preserved by keeping the island hidden from the public in a veil of secrecy. People worship the gods that dwell on Okinoshima from afar and have long observed strict taboos limiting access to the island that remain in force today. All ships and ferries maintain a respectful distance from Okinoshima.

In the past, a handful of select visitors were permitted onto the island during special festivals after purifying themselves by bathing naked in the sea to rid themselves of all impurities. But even that custom has ceased.

Nowhere is as desirable as a place that forbids visitors. To satisfy this urge Okitsu-miya Yohaisho Worship Hall was built on a coastal terrace on the north side of nearby Oshima Island giving visitors an opportunity to view the sacred island from a reverential distance. On a clear day visitors to Okitsu-miya Yohaisho can see Okinoshima on the horizon.

Archaeological remains found on the island reveal five hundred years of ancient rituals, with artifacts dating from the fourth to the ninth centuries. Okitsu-miya, one of the three Munakata Taisha shrines, dominates the entire island.

The island's population consists of a single employee of the shrine – a Shinto priest, who is one of about two dozen Shinto priests who travel from the mainland by boat to man the island shrine on a rotational basis, praying and guarding against intruders.

Courtesy of: Imaki Hidekazu
© World Heritage Promotion Committee

Okinoshima Miare Festival みあれ祭.
The Munakata Taisha Shrine's Autumn
Festival takes place from 1-3 October. This
is a ritual that is enacted mainly at sea to
welcome the goddesses from Oshima Fishing
Port to Konominato Fishing Port. It is a
dramatic event in which about 300 fishing
boats are led by two elaborately decorated
craft carrying a portable shrine. The boats
cruise around the sound between Oshima
Island, the ports and the mainland.

Courtesy of Imaki Hidekazu
© World Heritage Promotion Committee

SHIRAKAWA-GO
白川郷

Gassho-zukuri 合掌造 at Shirakawa-go are
houses called *minka* – built of wooden beams
and assembled to form a steep thatched
roof that resembles two praying hands.
These structures were built to suit the winter
environment in Shirakawa and also provide
work space for the area's sericulture.

Shirakawa-go is in the remote mountains of Gifu Prefecture in a wild, secluded area that sees some of Japan's heaviest snowfall, usually two or three metres each winter. In addition, Shirakawa is cut off from the rest of Japan by encircling mountains. Because of these factors, interaction with neighboring regions has always been limited. Yet, its seclusion created the conditions for the development of specific cultural practices, architecture, customs, folklore and social interaction. Its unique farmhouses, known as *Gassho-zukuri* 'praying hands', are famous for their traditional architecture, some of which are more than 250 years old. This building style was designed to withstand the heavy winter snow, the steep A-frame roofs constructed without nails – using only wood, straw and clay. Similar buildings can be seen in other Japanese prefectures though here they have triangular eaves resembling an open book propped up on its covers. *Minka* houses, built of wooden beams, were houses for farmers, artisans and merchants. The roofs and attics were designed to provide room for cultivating silkworms, as sericulture was the main industry of the village for centuries. The buildings face north and south to minimize wind resistance whilst controlling the sunlight hitting the roof to keep them cool in summer and warm in winter.

Ogimachi is the largest village in Shirakawa-go and a popular day trip from Takayama. In fact, many of the farmhouses have been converted into inns for overnight visitors as a way to help keep the locals in business and avoid urban flight. Shirakawa-go is a superb example of a preserved way of life adapted to its unique and unspoiled environment.

TOMIOKA SILK MILL
富岡製糸場

Tomioka Silk Mill was Japan's first modern silk factory for processing silkworm cocoons into raw silk. The mill was built as a model factory with the help of French specialists to improve the quality of silk produced in Japan through the use of modern machines. The Meiji government pushed forward the modernization of industry in order to help make Japan competitive with foreign countries. The export of raw silk was heavily backed and financed by the government. The mill comprises several buildings that have been preserved – the silk-reeling mill where silkworm cocoons are reeled into silk; the warehouses storing silk-worm cocoons and also Brunat House, home of the mill's French head manager Paul Brunat plus dormitories for French advisors and Japanese staff.

Tomioka was chosen for its position as a transportation hub for dispatching silk to the port of Yokohama. Availability of land to build such a large factory complex, plenty of fresh water (needed in raw silk production) and proximity to cold storage facilities, where silkworm eggs could be stored, were also important considerations. The mill played a crucial role in making Japanese silk an international trade commodity while establishing silk and textiles as the country's most important industry at the time. The delicate silk threads played a more powerful role than anyone could have imagined at the time as silk production was a precursor to Japan's later industrial juggernauts. Leading Japanese car makers are connected to the textile industry: Toyota had its roots in the loom-making business, while Nissan's engines evolved from silk-reeling machines. In this way, silk production was the beginning of Japan's transition into heavy industry and cutting edge technology.

SHIRAKAMI SANCHI
白神山地

Shirakami Sanchi is a vast primeval beech forest in the far north of Japan. The main feature of the Shirakami Sanchi is the mountainous landscape through which rivers have cut deep gorges. It is home to unique plants and animals including protected species of black woodpeckers, serows and golden eagles. It was designated as Japan's first natural World Heritage site in 1993 for its virgin beech tree forest – one of the last natural beech forests left in Asia.

Many beech forests around the world lost much of their ecological diversity due to the formation of continental glaciers two million years ago. They survived in this part of Japan because continental glaciation did not occur. Beech trees are highly resistant to the weight of heavy snow, allowing these trees to survive the huge snowfalls along the Sea of Japan. Thanks to Shirakami Sanchi and an active movement to preserve primeval forests, these habitats still thrive.

Anmon Waterfall is one of the main attractions with a dramatic three-step series of falls. Although there is an entry procedure that must be followed before being allowed into the core, strictly protected part of the World Heritage Area, there is no need to book ahead to enjoy the hike up to Anmon Falls.

One more feature of the area is the Matagi people who still hunt, cut wood and conduct religious activities in Shirakami Sanchi in accordance with their ancient traditions. These mountain folk conduct these activities only for their subsistence, in stark contrast to commercial logging and other human practices that have permanently altered ecosystems for the worse around the world.

Shirakami Sanchi Beech Forest 白神山地ブナ 原生林 is one of the largest primeval forests of beech trees on earth and it is home to a vast variety of animals and plants. Its ecosystem is one of the few that has never been exposed to human activity. The forest floor has a deep humus layer created from the fallen leaves which acts like a sponge to keep rain water in the soil and, as a result, fresh spring water flows out of the ground.

Anmon-no-taki Waterfall 暗門の滝 is a series of three waterfalls formed by tributaries of the Inagi-gawa and Anmon-gawa rivers found along a 5km trekking course. These trails are surrounded by rock cliffs, and you can see beech, maple and pine trees. In winter the area is often closed because of heavy snowfall.

SHIRETOKO PENINSULA
知床半島

Those who imagine that Japan consists only of crowded cities and urban sprawl have never been to Shiretoko, tucked away in a remote part of northeast Hokkaido. The Shiretoko Peninsula is well known in Japan for its beautiful lakes, dramatic waterfalls and brown bears but it is much more than just that. It is also a nature preserve, one of the last pristine wildernesses remaining in Japan. Many endangered plants and animals thrive here thanks to measures put in place to protect them.

The Shiretoko Five Lakes are connected to each other by trails and a walkway. The area also has the world's largest population of wild brown bears. If bears are known to be active in the area, all the trails are shut down. Even though brown bears are vegetarian and not interested in humans unless annoyed, the threat of being attacked by a 400kg bear is not a pleasant one and stringent precautions are in place. There are more than thirty types of other wild and rare animals living in Shiretoko forests with over 250 known bird species including rare and endangered sea eagles. The ecosystem reflects the important linkage between the sea and the land and is thus is a very important wildlife reserve unlike any other.

Shiretoko Five Lakes 知床五湖 is a group of five small lakes formed by the eruption of nearby Mount Io. Water is fed into the lakes by underground springs. The lakes offer beautiful views of the surrounding mountains and wilderness and provide visitors with an easy way to experience the abundance of Hokkaido's unspoiled nature. An elevated boardwalk was constructed for viewing the lakes without damaging the ecosystem, and to protect visitors from wild brown bears that live in the area. There are also ground-level nature trails, though going with a guide is usually mandatory.

Shiretoko Peninsula 知床半島. The Shiretoko Peninsula is well known in Japan for its beautiful lakes, dramatic waterfalls and unusual rock formations by the sea, but it is much more than that. It is also a nature preserve of untouched wilderness, thanks to its remote location and strict protection measures to keep it that way.

Godzila Rock ゴジラ岩. Oronko-iwa Rock and Sankaku-iwa Rock are picturesque rock or island formations around the tip of Cape Utoro. These huge rocks, and Oronko-iwa Rock in particular, are well-known spots for sunset viewing. A wooden stairway is built from the trailhead to the top of the rock. Godzilla Rock lies more inland, and to the Japanese imagination appears to be Godzilla rising from the sea.

Brown Bears ヒグマ. Shiretoko is well known for having one of the highest brown bear populations in the world. During certain periods of the year the bears come out and hiking trails are closed after bear sightings. The best and safest way to view the brown bears is by boat along the Shiretoko coastline. Certain boats are devoted exclusively to bear watching.

NATIONAL MUSEUM OF WESTERN ART
国立西洋美術館

Tokyo has been the official capital of Japan since 1868 when it was renamed from Edo to Tokyo when the Meiji Emperor moved all functions there. As a result of this fairly recent history, there are few World Heritage monuments in Tokyo.

Tokyo can boast of one unusual World Heritage site, however, namely the special architecture of the National Museum of Western Art in Ueno Park. The building was designed by Charles-Édouard Jeanneret, otherwise known as Le Corbusier. The museum was added as a world heritage site along with sixteen other Corbusier projects around the world for its significant architecture and historical associations. The museum was originally set up to house the personal collection of Matsukata Kojiro and contains the work of Manet, Rodin, Picasso and Pollock. This landmark also celebrates the renewal of diplomatic relations between France and Japan after World War II.

Seventeen buildings in seven countries by the Swiss-French architect were registered collectively. These seventeen buildings were constructed over a period of fifty years. The buildings' designs reflect solutions that the modernist movement sought to apply during the 20th century. They also reflect the challenge of creating new architectural techniques to respond to the changing needs of society. This collection of architectural masterpieces pays tribute to the creative genius in the internationalization of architectural practices across the globe. The functionalist Le Corbusier also had a poetic side. One of Le Corbusier's key ideas was to create a 'museum of unlimited growth' – which is to say a structure that could be expanded with additional external rooms as the collection grew. NMWA regularly holds exhibitions by the most renowned names in the history of art and is the foremost public art gallery in Japan specializing in European art.

OGASAWARA ISLANDS
小笠原諸島

Ogasawara Islands were once known as the Bonin Islands and were formed about 48 million years ago by volcanos. Although people speak of Ogasawara as though it is one large island, it is in fact a chain of some thirty islands. Its main islands are Chichijima 'Father Island' and Hahajima 'Mother Island', the only ones that are inhabited with a total population of 2500 people.

The islands are 1000km away from Tokyo but are a part of Tokyo City – even sharing the same postal code. Yet in every sense the islands are about as far away from Tokyo as it is possible to get. This is the domain of frolicking dolphins, whales, boobies and the albatross – not buttoned-down businessmen forever in a rush. The main port is the village of Omura on Chichijima, which far more resembles ramshackle villages in Okinawa or Hawaii rather than metropolitan Tokyo.

Plant and animal life was transported to the islands by ocean currents, winds or birds and settled on the Islands undergoing a unique process of evolution. The rare fauna and flora have developed through a unique evolutionary process particular to isolated island ecosystems with many endemic species. Because of this Ogasawara is sometimes referred to as the 'Galapagos of the Orient'. Ogasawara is a place where one can feel the heartbeat of the East and its creatures. Fauna include the Bonin Flying Fox and 195 endangered birds including the rare Laysan albatross. Flora such as *Pandanus boninensis* and *Rhododendron boninense* are only found here. The islands' beaches are some of the very best in Japan with crystal clear water, lack of crowds, and pristine corals and ocean life.

Minamijima Island 南島 is an uninhabited island southwest of Chichijima. Visiting the island is strictly regulated to protect and preserve its environment and native ecosystems. Only 100 visitors are allowed to enter per day and must be accompanied by a guide. The most beautiful place on Minamijima Island is Ougiike, which is both a lagoon and gateway to the island. It serves as an icon of Ogasawara because of its unique lagoon cave with an opening framing the ocean beyond. Minamijima was formed by submerged karst as most of the landscape sank beneath the ocean due to crustal movement. This landscape is so unique and rare that it is designated as a natural monument.

Rhododendron boninense Nakai

A plant species endemic to the Ogasawara Isalnds. Most species have brightly colored flowers. The most common variety are azaleas which are distinguished from true rhododendrons by having only five anthers per flower as opposed to ten.

Pandanus boninensis

Sometimes called a screw pine, because of its unusual roots, this species of pandan is endemic to the Ogasawara Islands. Two unusual and unique triterpenoids and alkaloids that may be useful in medicines have been isolated from the leaves of *Pandanus boninensis.*

Yatsusegawa river trail

Ogasawara has many nature trails for spotting rare plant species and bird watching. Most of the trails are reserved sanctuaries requiring a licensed guide to enter. One of the few trails that allows the solo adventurer is the Yatsusegawa River Trail where visitors can breathe nature in its abundance with hardly any other souls nearby, despite its being next door to one of the very best beaches in Japan.

Snail fossils, Minamijima

One of the most unusual attractions at Minamijima are the fossils of snails that became extinct over 1000 years ago. They are half buried on the sandy shores of the island. These unique fossils can be seen easily but visitors are not permitted to touch them or any other animals or plants on the island.

Laysan albatross

This is a bird endemic to the Ogasawara Islands and is found only in the Pacific Ocean. These large seabirds with exceptional flying skills can cover long distances by using dynamic soaring. Certain species of albatross are recognized as the oldest wild birds in the world and are considered to be endangered or vulnerable.

Green sea turtle

These turtles are found throughout the world, usually in tropical waters, but were in a steep decline since the 1970s because of the harvesting of turtles and their eggs. Their population has grown over the past 30 years after strict worldwide protection began. There are several hotspots in Ogasawara where sea turtles lay their eggs.

NAGASAKI 長崎

Nagasaki, like Hiroshima, is known world-wide for its modern historical significance. However, Nagasaki's history resonates with other famous chapters in Japanese and world history. Opera fans will recognize immed-iately the strains of Puccini's *Madame Butterfly*, set in Nagasaki. But even before this, Nagasaki was Japan's window on the world for more than 200 years, when the rest of the country was closed off and in isolation. During this period, the Dutch were allowed to stay, albeit sequestered on their own little island in Nagasaki harbor complete with their own church. Nagasaki's Chinese population in nearby Chinatown also main-tained links with the outside world during this time. Consequently, unlike any other city in Japan, Nagasaki has several layers of culture, taste and history all set in a hilly bayside town with rattling streetcars, the sound of foghorns and sea breezes as ships docked into port.

Kyushu and Nagasaki, in particular, were proselytizing grounds for Christians, even Jesuit missionary Francis Xavier paid a visit.

In its early stages, Christianity was tolerated, but in the 16th century a strict ban on Christianity in Japan was issued. During this period, there was mass persecution of Christians and many churches were destroyed. The religion became illegal and was severely punished. Many Japanese Christians went into hiding, were tortured or killed, while missionaries were deported. By 1640 not a single priest, either European or Japanese, was left in Japan. Nevertheless, many Japanese Christians persisted in practicing their religion in secret during the ban.

When the ban was lifted during the Meiji Restoration, Christian churches sprang up in previous enclaves of secret Christians in the Nagasaki prefecture – most of which were in remote offshore Goto Islands. In these places churches were built in the 1800s to commemorate those who had been martyred for their faith. Oura Church in central Nagasaki and Tabira Church in Hirado are excellent examples of the recon-struction of these Christian hopes in the Nagasaki Prefecture.

Oura Cathedral 大浦天主堂 is a Roman Catholic church in Nagasaki. It is also known as the Church of the 26 Japanese Martyrs in memory of the 26 Christians killed in 1597. It was established by a French missionary and is the only Western-style building declared a national treasure. Oura claims to be the oldest church in Japan and has been recognized by the Vatican as a minor basilica for its important historical value.

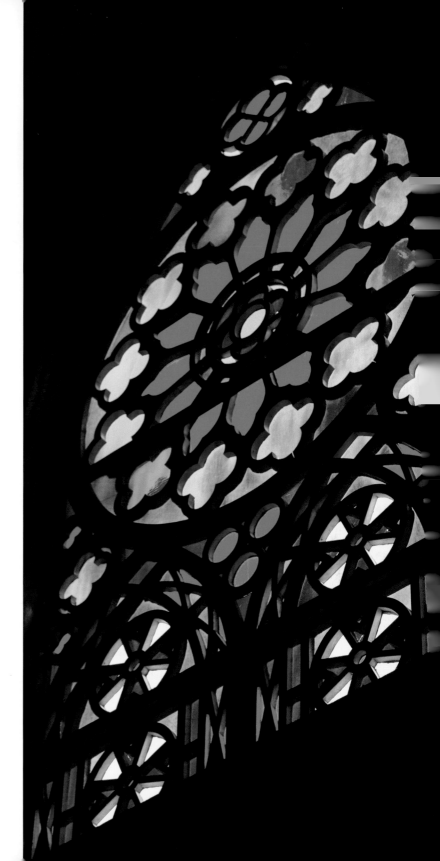

Tabira Church 田平天主堂 *(left)*. The history of Tabira began with French missionary Emile Raguet who in 1886 purchased two acres of wilderness at his own expense and arranged to settle Japanese Christian families on his land. The same year, Marc-Marie de Rotz bought additional land and sent more families to live nearby and the number of settlers increased steadily. In 1914 Japanese priest Nakata Tokichi raised funds for a formal church with the parishioners helping with its construction. Tabira Church is distinctive with its three-story central tower protruding from the front with an octagonal dome belfry. The building faces the Hirado Strait and has been designated an important cultural asset by the Japanese government.

Egami Church 江上天主堂 *(above)*. In 1918 descendants of the Goto island settlers helped build the church under the direction of Tetsukawa Yosuke. Egami Village on Naru Island is part of the Hidden Christian legacy of migrants from the mainland who continued to practise their faith secretly during the ban on Christianity. Egami Church is considered to be the best example in terms of design and structure among the wooden church buildings built in the region of Nagasaki from the 19th century onwards.

Former Gorin Church 旧五輪教会堂 was built in 1881 and is the second oldest church after Oura Church in Nagasaki. In 1931 Hamawaki Church was rebuilt with a larger space to replace the wooden structure. The restored church uses a rare combination of Japanese and Western construction methods. It has an outer appearance of a traditional Japanese building but an interior consisting of a nave with two aisles and boarded rib-vault ceilings. It is no longer a church, but is maintained by Goto City, and is a part of the UNESCO World Heritage Nagasaki Hidden Christian sites.

Dozaki Church Bas-Relief 堂崎教会堂 レリーフ.
Dozaki Church, built by French missionaries is
the oldest church in the Goto Islands, Nagasaki.
It now serves as a museum displaying items related
to the 300-year suppression of Christianity in
Japan and was designated as a Tangible Cultural
Asset of Nagasaki Prefecture in 1974. In 1879, a
temporary chapel was constructed here by Father
Marmand of the Paris Foreign Mission Society.
In the decades following freedom, churches were
built across the archipelago by communities of
hidden Christians. On Fukue, the first Western-
style church to be built was red-brick Dozaki,
completed in its present form in 1908. The bas-
relief shows a meeting of the hidden Christians.

TENTATIVE
SITES
暫定リスト

UNESCO's selection criterion for inclusion to the World Heritage sites is rigorous and requires enormous cooperation among the parties nominating the sites. Certain values must be present: cultural and natural heritage or mixed cultural and natural heritage, cultural landscapes, movable heritage and outstanding universal value.

Hikone Castle is one of the few castles to have made it to the tentative list as it is one of the rare ones that have not been extensively renovated and retains its original form, along with its feudal period garden at its foot. Although not as grand and imposing as Himeji Castle, Hikone gets points for the purity of its original architectural form – it has only had minor repairs made to it over the centuries. Hikone-jo has also been designated as a National Treasure of Japan and its adjacent garden Genkyu-an was chosen as a Place of Scenic Beauty by the Japanese government.

The area around Asuka in the Nara Prefecture is considered to be the cradle of Japanese civilization. It is here where the first emperors of Japan established their seats of power and where many of the remains of Japan's oldest stone monuments, tombs and archeological excavations can be found. The Ishibutai Tumulus is an impressive yet mysterious megalith believed to be the tomb of Soga no Umako, a powerful figure during the Asuka period. At first it was thought to be a performance stage but a sarcophagus was found inside during later excavations. Nearby Kameishi Turtle Rock, Takamatsu-zaka Tumulus and Murals are the main features of Asuka.

Kamakura, the ancient capital, is thought of by most Japanese today as a pleasant beach town, as it is only 50km from Tokyo. Apart from Shonan Beach, the icons of Kamakura are Tsurugaoka Shrine with its massive *torii* gates and frequent festivals, weddings and events. Further up the hill is ancient Kenchoji, Zuisenji and Engakuji temples but the greatest of them all – the Daibutsu, the Great Buddha of Kamakura is one of the largest bronze statues of Buddha in the world. Apart from the temples, gardens and shrines Kamakura has a special circuit of hiking trails with caves and carved stone passes. These trails were originally meant to connect the temples to each other; adding a natural attraction that is a welcome retreat from the sprawl of nearby Tokyo.

Kamakura: Home of the Samurai has been on the tentative list since 1992, but it has temporarily dropped out of the running for inclusion, and is presently revising its bid for UNESCO nomination. Even so, 'temples, shrines and other structures of Ancient Kamakura' officially remain on the UNESCO tentative list, for the time being.

Hikone
彦根

Hikone Castle 彦根城. Hikone-jo was completed in 1622 after 20 years of construction, using materials from nearby castles which had been torn down. It was finally finished by Ii Naokatsu. The Ii family remained allies of the ruling Tokugawa Shogunate throughout the Edo period. The castle is an ornate black and white fortress and was the base of the local Ii family *daimyo* (feudal lord) of the area. The top of the keep has wonderful views on a clear day over the surrounding countryside and Lake Biwa. Hikone-jo retains its original buildings, unlike many Japanese castles that have been rebuilt.

Genkyu-en 玄宮園 at Hikone Castle is a feudal-period garden located below Hikone-jo, created to resemble the Eight Views of Lake Biwa. Such landscape gardens have a central pond and circular paths. Genkyu-en was built by the local lord for the entertainment of his guests and family. It was modeled after a palace garden from Tang Dynasty China. There are four small islands dotted around the pond, connected by bridges. On the shore of the pond garden stands the Rakurakuen Palace that served as the secondary residence for the lord's family.

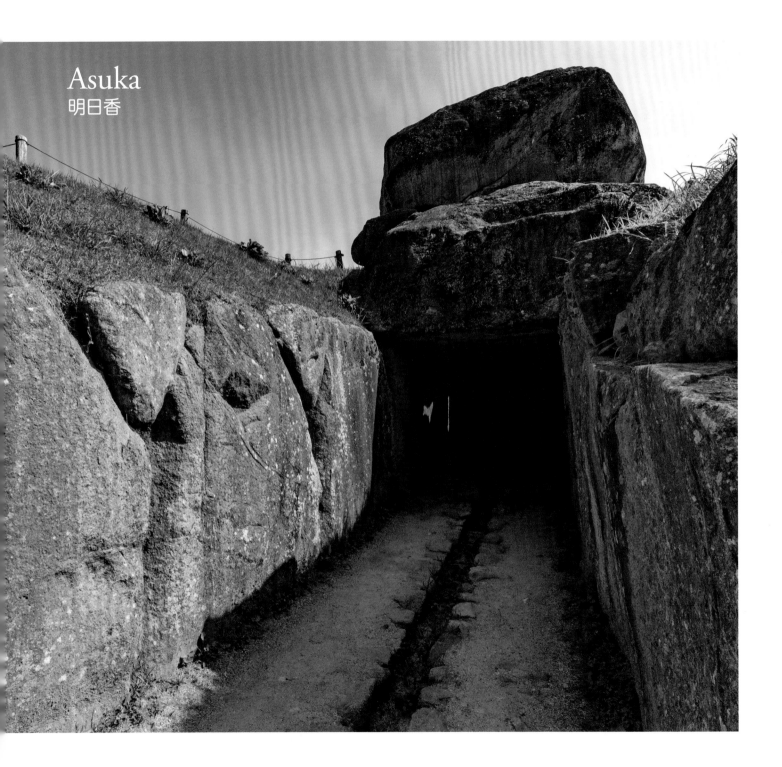

Asuka

明日香

Ishibutai Tumulus 石舞台古墳. The Ishibutai tumulus was first excavated in 1933 but at that time little was discovered as it had been pilfered by grave robbers. Further investigation found that it had been a large tomb of an emperor and that it is the largest megalithic structure in Japan. Once inside the tomb chamber, visitors are in awe of the huge stones that form the walls and high ceiling, and wonder how they got there.

Takamatsuzuka Tumulus Burial Mound
高松塚壁画 is a stone burial chamber containing a sarcophagus. The walls, ceiling and floor inside the stone chamber are decorated with murals, which were discovered in 1972. The tumulus itself is a special historic site and the four-colored murals are national treasures. Their discovery has influenced Japanese archaeology, ancient history and art history. Although the original murals are not normally available for public viewing, replicas are displayed in the Takarazuka Mural Hall next to the burial mound.

Kameishi Turtle Rock 亀石. Several Kameishi turtle stones can be found in Japan, including at Shizuoka and Sado Island, but the best known is in Asuka. This granite megalith was carved into the shape of a tortoise facing south, although legend has it that it originally faced east and if it ever turned to face the west, all of Japan would be reduced to a sea of mud. The Kameishi Turtle Rock in Asuka, along with other nearby megaliths and tombs, have been identified as an ancient star chart mapping the constellation of Cassiopeia, known as Five Emperors by the Chinese.

Takamatsuzuka Murals 高松塚壁画 are covered with images of a turtle entwined with a snake, a blue dragon, figures of the sun and tigers. On the ceiling there is an early chart of the constellations. The murals were made by covering stone surfaces with plaster, then drawing outlines, followed by coloring in the drawings. The refined coloring and delicate lines render the figures of human, beast and dieties full of character and vitality. Because of the disintegration of these ancient murals, they have had to be carefully removed and restored.

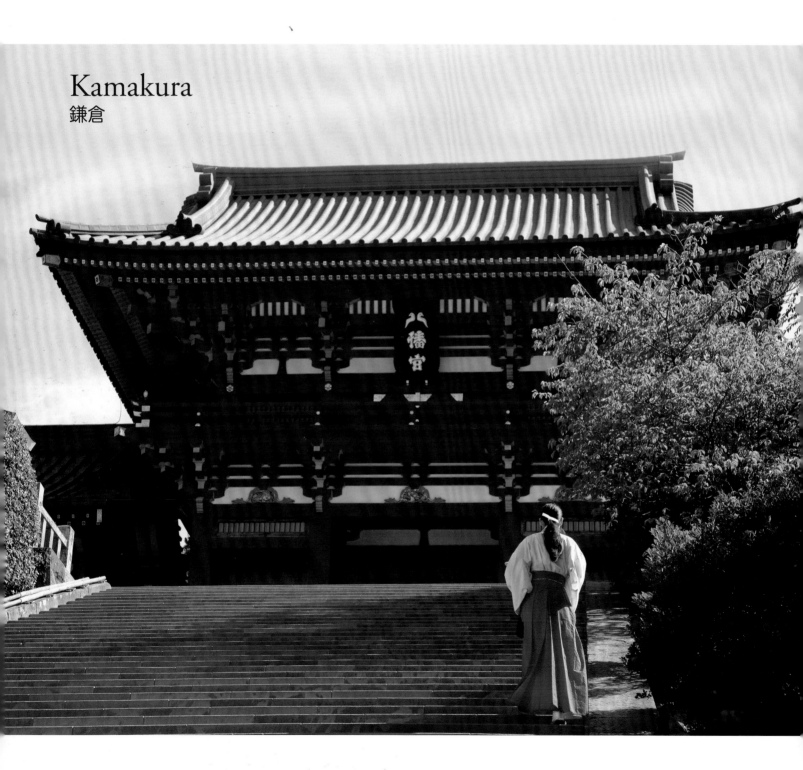

Kamakura
鎌倉

Tsurugaoka Hachimiangu Shrine 鶴岡八幡 is the most important Shinto shrine in Kamakura, as well one of the most prominent in Kanagawa Prefecture. Although it is now a Shinto shrine, Tsurugaoka Hachiman-gu was a Buddhist temple for most of its history. Most ceremonies and festivals in Kamakura are held here, including weddings and Coming of Age day in January.

The Great Buddha of Kamakura 鎌倉大仏. This monumental bronze statue of Buddha was cast by Ono Goroemon in 1253, a leading craftsman of his time. There are traces of gold leaf near the statue's ears as the entire figure was originally gilded. The hall in which the Daibutsu was housed was destroyed by a typhoon in 1334, rebuilt, then damaged once again by yet another storm in 1369. It was rebuilt a third time, but the last building washed away in the tsunami of September 1498. Since then, the Great Buddha has stood in the open, as it does today. Daibutsu is located within the grounds of Kotoku-in Temple.

Kenchojji 建長寺 is the oldest Zen monastery in Japan, built in the Kamakura period in 1273. The layout of the temple follows the Chinese Xian tradition with all the buildings arranged on an axis. It is known for its architecture, especially its golden gates. Also, there is an austere pond garden – one of the few Japanese gardens in Kamakura. Kenchoji is one of the Five Great Zen Temples of Kamakura. While still important and occupying a large amount of space, in its heyday it housed 49 sub-temples. During the Kamakura period, scholars from the Five Great Zen Temples exercised great power in Japan.

Nagoe Kiridoshi Pass 名越切通 was built as an important pathway into Kamakura. The pass was considered as protection and defense during the Kamakura period as intruders were obstructed. Along the trail there are caves that were once used as burial sites. Access to Kamakura has always been difficult, bordered by mountains on three sides and the ocean on the other. These passes were essential for transport, but at the same time gave limited access as horses could not squeeze through such narrow trails. Kamakura Kiridoshi Passes are thought to have been constructed in the early 13th century.

Shomyoji 称名寺 was built by Hojo Sanetoki during the Kamakura period and was the Hojo family temple. The Jodo-style Pure Land garden with Ajiike Pond in front of the main temple is its most unique feature and the arched bridge its highlight. The temple's bell was portrayed in the woodblock print *Shomyo-no-Bansho,* one of eight prints depicting views of Kanazawa by Hiroshige Utagawa. Today Shomyoji is no longer part of Kamakura but is officially within Yokohama city limits.

Notes

Further information
JNTO Japan National Travel Organization
www.jnto.go.jp

Bibliography / Further reading
The Kojiki: An Account of Ancient Matters
Gustav Heldt, 2014
Columbia University Press
ISBN 9780231163897

A Concise History of Japan
Brett L Walker, 2015
Cambridge University Press
ISBN 9780521178723

Lafcadio Hearn's Japan
Donald Ritchie, 2007
Tuttle
ISBN 9784805308738

Japan's World Heritage Sites
John Dougill, 2014
Tuttle
ISBN 9784805312858

Glossary
Asuka period 538 to 710
Nara period 710-794
Heian period 794-1185 (most of it in Kyoto)
Kamakura period 1185-1333
Kenmu restoration period 1333-1336
Muromachi period 1336-1573
Edo period 1603-1868
Meiji period 1868-1912
Taisho period 1912-1926
Showa period 1926-1989

Daimyo
Feudal lord, vassals of shogun.

Edo
Archaic word for Tokyo, meaning 'eastern capital'.

Gasho-zukuri
A-frame buildings, that are thought to resemble praying hands, with steep eaves to prevent heavy snows from collapsing the roofs.

Henro
Buddhist pilgrim, especially those found on the Shikoku Pilgrimage and at Koyasan.

Ijinkan
Westernstyle house, usually Meiji period.

Jizo
Bodhisattva depicted as a Buddhist monk but is in fact a guardian of children, women and travelers.

Jo
Castle: Himeji Castle referred to as Himeji-jo.

Kanji
Chinese characters used in the Japanese writing system.

Karesansui
Dry landscape garden, usually called a Zen garden' outside of Japan.

Koan
Puzzling or paradoxical statement to inspire introspection in Zen Buddhism.

Minka
Minka are vernacular buildings and usually the dwellings of farmers, with thatched roofs.

Nagare zukuri
Architectural style with an asymetrical roof projecting outwards.

Onsen
Hot springs, of which there are thousands in Japan.

Rakan
Buddha's disciples usually in the form of sculptures.

San
Honorific word, usually used for people: 'John-san' but sometimes for venerated objects such as Mount Fuji 'Fuji-san'.

Shakkei
The principle of using background landscape in the composition of a garden.

Shichi-go-san
Literally 7, 5, 3 is a tradition where children of those ages visit their family shrine on 15 November, an auspicious day, to pray for the healthy growth of children.

Shinto: the original religion of Japan
Shrines are often found within the grounds of Buddhist temples, adding to the confusion of non-Japanese.

Shogun
Rulers of Japan during the Tokugawa Shogunate, during Nara and Heian periods.

Torii
Gates to a Shinto shrine, usually vermilion in color.

Tsukubai
Water basin found at temples to purify oneself before entering temple compounds.

Notable people

Matsuo Basho
Wandering haiku poet, the most famous from the Edo period.

Kobo Daishi
Scholar, poet, traveler, civil servant and Buddhist monk who founded Shingon Esoteric Buddhist, also known as Kukai.

Soami
Tea ceremony master, poet, painter and designer of some of Japan's most renowned gardens.

Kobori Enshu
Tea ceremony master, aristocrat, artist and designer of some of Japan's most renowned gardens.

Muso Soseki
Prominent Zen Buddhist abbot, calligrapher, poet writer and presumed designer of some of Japan's most renowned gardens.

Hayao Miyazaki
Co-founder of Studio Ghibli, an animation studio that produced movie 'Princess Mononoke' set in Yakushima.

Tokugawa
The Tokugawa shogunate, beginning with Ieyasu Tokugawa ruled Japan from 1600 until 1868. The period of rule is called the Tokugawa period or Edo period as their seat of power was Edo, now called Tokyo.

Emperor Meiji
The Meiji period marks the move from Japan as a feudal society towards an industrialized empire. In its early days it was seen as a time of enlightenment.